LIBRARY DATABASE MANAGEMENT

LIBRARY DATABASE MANAGEMENT

Editor
Arunaima Baruah

KALPAZ PUBLICATIONS
Delhi–110 052

LIBRARY DATABASE MANAGEMENT
Library and Information Science

Rs. 775

ISBN: 81-7835-085-8

Published in 2002 in India by
Kalpaz Publications
C–30, Satyawati Nagar
Ashok Vihar Phase–III
Delhi–110 052
E-mail: Kalpaz@hotmail.com

Printed at: Mehra Offset Printers, New Delhi

Preface

The communication networks is expanding continuously. Despite the considerable implications that most of the wide, metropolitan, and local area networks are ineffective and frequently fail, database management receives too little attention. One reason is that computer systems and communication networks have reached a level of complexity and power that exceeds human abilities to understand, predict, and thus, manage. The only way to change this situation is to critical success factors of database management, which include database management functions, instruments, and human resources.

All relevant configuration and performance data may be centrally stored and maintained using existing data bases or files. The network-management-oriented data may be integrated or kept separate. A certain group of customers may directly access this data base. Particular care should be taken, however, to assure that the performance of productive type of work will not be impaired. Program-to-program links may be used for completing, problem related records, as part of the trouble file. There is a frequent discussion about what kind of data should be maintained in a network-management data base. The following list of components consider an average installation.

For successful database management, related data should be continuously collected in all principal network components. This information is preprocessed and used for different purpose in operational, tactical, and strategic database management.

The primary object of this book is to provide a detailed practical guideline for corporations and professionals in the area of library database management. Librarians, network managers, planners and administrators, tele-communication managers, analysts, and operators are the primary audience. The information provided is valuable for information systems managers as well.

Editor

Contents

1

Database Management

A communication system consists of all system-related components. A component is defined as anything that, when not functioning properly, impacts the end customer. Included are terminals, modems, lines, multiplexers, storage devices, processors, system software, and application software used to support a network. Also included are the sources of power, air-conditioning, water chillers and numerous operational procedures, because their failures may also impact the end user.

Communication networks can operate properly only when all management areas and components are satisfactorily addressed. The component indicated include hardware, system application and communication software. In order to reduce the time between failures and their restoration, unique procedures should be prepared prior to installation. Using the mainstream concept, these procedures should be centrally distributed and maintained. They are invoked by certain types of solicited or unsolicited messages.

Depending on the definition of span of control, network outages may be reported to one location only.

The processing power in one or more of the host computers provide sufficient support for the management tasks. The information gathered at remote sites is usually time-division multiplexed onto the productive circuits. Using processors that already support application may accommodate special purpose management tasks. Thus, additional hardware can be saved. However, the overhead involved should be carefully evaluated and controlled.

All relevant configuration and performance data may be centrally stored and maintained using existing data bases or files. The network-management-oriented data may be integrated or kept separate. A certain group of customers may directly access this data base. Particular care should be taken, however, to assure that the performance of productive type of work will not be impaired. Program-to-program links may be used for completing, problem related records, as part of the trouble file. There is a frequent discussion about what kind of data should be maintained in a network-management data base. The following list of components consider an average installation. The final decision, however, depends on

— Required information resolution

— Tools implemented

— Database responsibilities for supporting network management.

The most important components are:

— The data dictionary provides an overview about all information stored in the network-management data base. The amount of information stored may be customized.

— Identification fields are used for unique classification of all information stored. They may he categorised by application groups:

Batch:	Job name
	Accounting fields Job class
	RJE station identification
	Programmer name
Time sharing:	User identification
	Accounting fields
Data base:	User identification
	Transaction codes
	Terminal identification
TP-monitor:	User identification
	Transaction codes
	Terminal identification

General workload and traffic volumes indicate quantities at a global level for a certain period of time. They usually include

1) Link level (transactions, messages)
   - — IN
   - — OUT
   - — Byte count
2) Network level
   - — Null-header packets
   - — Non-null-header packets
   - — Byte count
3) Transport level
   - — Number of connections (in, out)
   - — Number of requests

— Number of expedited transactions or messages (in, out)

— Byte count

4) Session level

— Number of accepted connections

— Number of rejected connections

— Byte count

5) Application level (node oriented)

— Number of jobs, transactions, messages

— Number of net and control characters

Further processing the indicators for averaging, calculating peak-average ratios, and percentiles is usually supported.

— Resource utilization measures indicate actual and average utilization profiles for a certain period of time. Profiles usually included are

Nodes

Processing unit

Busy

Problem

Supervisor

Wait

Protection key

Memory

I/O area

Channel busy

Byte count

- Controller busy
- Device busy
- Contention

Links

- Busy/wait
- Bytes transferred
- Bytes received
- Retransmission
- Timeout

Overlapping

- Processors and I/O
- Processors and communication
- Wait for I/O
- Wait for communication

Service-level measures give an overview of the service provided, frequently offering comparison for the actual level with planned over predefined time windows. Indicators included are:

Availability

- Hardware level
- System level
- Application level
- Session level
- Transport level
- Network level
- Link level
- Physical level

Customer level

Basis information is provided by trouble tickets.

Response time

Node delay

Link delay

User-think time

Response-time distribution by

User

Workstation

Cluster

Line

Communication controller

Node

Application

Accuracy and integrity

Application

Transfer

Session

Connection

Network

Link

— Application unit measures classify the principal workload clusters for workload characterisation and repre-sentation. There are numerous alternative, but the most frequently used include

Production (data base, transaction, monitor, infocenter, batch)

Test (data base, transaction, monitor, infocenter, batch, program development)

Systems support (housekeeping, utilities)

— Configuration describes the inventory-control and topological data.

The most frequently used entries are

Nodes

Names, addresses, and directories

Classification (source, destination, relay, LAN)

Identification (code, model, location)

Application support

Reliability (trouble reports, MTBF)

Throughput

Vendor (name, address, phone, responsibility)

Software implemented (e.g., IMS, CICS, VTAM, NCP, TIPX, TELCON, PDN, EXPAND, CNS, etc.)

Compression software implemented

Connectivity

Maintenance

Recovery rules

Auditability

Links

Names, addresses, and directories

Architecture and topology for network and/ or for subnetworks

Source destination connections

Speed

Procedure (character, bit or asynchronous)

Modus (simplex, half- or full-duplex)

Links identification and performance indicators

- Communication line
- Microwave
- Lightwave
- Satellite

Connectivity

Maintenance

Recovery rules

Auditability

Value-added service identification and performance

- Packet switching
- Line switching
- Message switching
- Electronic mail
- Teleconferencing
- Voice mail
- Videotex
- ISDN

Vendor (name, address, telephone, responsibility, contracts)

All entries include inventory status, such as operational, ordered, and change logs, sorted by the inventory identification connectivity (physical connections of the components to each other at the paths for end-to-end and application-application levels) Circuits (physical connections specified by the connectivity constitute logical circuits between applications and end-user nodes)

— Software classification used for describing both application and system software related characteristics. They include the following items:

Inventory of installed and in-process software (ID, name, status)

Supplier

Ownership

Security (access and physical) Recovery rules

Auditability

Connectivity requirements

Maintenance requirements

— Customer information describes vital customer-related data such as addresses, telephone numbers, and application-access authorization service requirements.

— Both open and closed *trouble tickets* should become part of the data base. In addition, compressed versions of closed trouble tickets can be included. They are interrogated by operational control during problem determination. Status and resolution of open tickets are usually interrogated by network administration. Usual information includes problem definition, impacts, status, severity, responsibility, maintenance, and tuning request.

— Ordering and billing information can be included optionally. Such information may be correlated with inventory status, financial data, and accounting information.

— Security logs may be included optionally for interrogating and further processing security violations, evaluating unusual occurrences, improving the security plan, and triggering alarms by certain types of violations.

— Communication system overhead measures may be included as well. Some of them are measurable, but some of them are not yet. Measured overhead profiles include

Telecommunication-access methods

Telecommunication monitors such as

CICS

Com-Plete

Task-Master

Shadow

Protocol overhead, such as

Character-oriented

Bit-oriented

Asynchronous

Special compression software overhead

Not-yet-measurable communication overhead includes:

NCP/PEP/EP/Telcon

Monitoring features

NPA/NPM	NETVIEW
NPDA	PDN
NLDM	WSNMON
VNCA	COMALERT

OBSERVER

Management features

CMC	NET/MASTER
HCF	NMS
DSX	TNAS
DMF	

Overhead indicators have to be considered by network-capacity planning tor calculating the realistic resource demand of communication and processing.

— Natural forecast units (NFUs) are relevant for predicting the future resource demand and transaction-arrival rates as a function of business-related forecasts. NFUs could be the number of checks, number of passengers, number of reservations, number of tires manufactured, number of inquiries, or number of reports generated, depending on the industry and the size of the organization. Very frequently, multiple NFUs should be considered until the most important ones can be determined by means of a dependency analysis.

The customer can extend this nucleus at any time. The most promising way is to start with existing files and link them together using external products or home grown procedures. For successful management of large data-processing shops, the information demand for the following should be satisfied in a timely manner:

— Operational control

— Administration of data-processing and communication equipment

— Performance analysis

— Capacity planning

In many shops, tile basic data are available somewhere in some form, but retrieving them is very cumbersome. There is an information management problem because of the following:

— Too much data collected and saved due to improper choice of sampling rate.

— Too many products implemented and evaluated.

— Too many reports generated on a permanent basis for all management levels without careful consideration of actual need.

— Expense of products and staffing for extracting and analysing information.

— Redundancy among the products.

— Multiple autark data bases without correliability.

— For ad-hoc inquiries, correlations and displays, the speed of internal processing of data bases is not sufficient.

— Expense of compute. resources for collecting, storing, processing, and reporting performance-related information

To improve overall efficiency in the area of managing network management-related information there is a definite need for a comprehensive data base system. Information sour include network technical-control systems, network monitors, electronic switches, features of the communication software, software monitors and special purpose measurement devices. Thus, validity checks can be accomplished by the Information Translator prior to being accepted for the data base. Arriving information is converted into the database internal format by the Information Translator. There is always a trade-off when defining the proper database structure. On one side, there are the requirements for total flexibility; on the other side, however, performance criteria should be taken into account.

For analysing information requirements, data elements can be organized into network structure, but several groups of data frequently demanded together can also be structured in a hierarchical way. Recent evaluations show the applicability of relational and object-oriented storage of information. In particular, the object-oriented organizational form is preferenced by artificial intelligence, promising outstanding user interfaces by high performance.

Internal data conversion and data preprocessing is accomplished by the Data Base Organiser. Using the network-management database, user requirements have to be met. The Report Administrator is responsible for report generation. The different parameters, such as frequency, threshold values, time of generation, output form, and so on, can be defined by using several input features. In order not to impair overall database flexibility, data should be processed only when required.

The processing includes complete arithmetic and logic functions on data items, conditional and unconditional branching, editing, data conversion, change of sequence of computations, mathematical functions, update, sort, merge, match, and word manipulations. As emphasized previously, the system operates using the reporting- by-exception technique. Thus, the Administrator is activated in most cases in the interactive way or by predefined states. In order to reduce specification efforts, frequently required procedures can be catalogued. But this option should not impair Information Access (first of all special-inquiry requirements) in any way. In addition to routine outputs, detailed processing is very often required. In some cases, one may be interested in statistical evaluation of correlation between resource utilization and workload components. For such purposes, application programs are designed that use database components as their own parts. This feature is accomplished by the programmer Interface. In addition, parts of the data base can be compressed and dumped onto a temporary display data base. This data base can be physically located on a personal computer as well.Depending on the installation's conventions, the processing schedules should be decided upon. Currently, the majority of performance and accounting-related information is provided via daily tapes, mostly SMF types for the IBM environment. Other sources are usually converted onto SMF format first.

In the future, on-line interfaces from information-extraction instruments are expected as well. Administration- related data are entered in dialogue. The maintenance of the data base must not be underestimated. Key success factors include:

— Determination of updates and compression intervals

— Allocation of responsibilities within the organization

— Determination of the number of database generations for recovery purposes

— Preparation of procedures for database crashes

— Working out update sequences and schedules

— Controlling missing-data intervals

A network management data base in the narrow sense should be evaluated by using the following criteria:

1. *Information sources*: How many and what kind of such as software, network, modem, application

and hardware monitors, can be understood. The more sources can be integrated, the better the chances for correlative analysis and reporting. Also included specific validation and context checks.

2. *Data volumes*: Efficient processing of large amounts of data may required for updates from multiple sources within given time intervals.
3. *Level of detail*: The capability of maintaining data at various levels of detail serves management as well as analysis. Usually, the level of details controlled by time.
4. *Update procedures*: The amounts of time and resources required for updates. In addition, requirement for automated updates may be included.
5. *Internal processing features*: Summarize requirements toward reduction, sort, selection, and creation of derived data elements. Access, availability, and performance issues are addressed here.
6. *Hardware/software dependency*: Answers whether the data base is dependent on hardware or software features of mainframe and/or monitor vendor.
7. *Demand*: Demand for adapting additional information sources and additional information segments, such as administration from the same or other vendors. It is a property of flexibility and expandability of the network-management data base in dynamically changing the networking environment.
8. *Relational capabilities*: Important for accelerating retrieval procedures during analysis and reporting, and more importantly during real-time conditions.

9. *Query language*: Powerful database query requires a user-friendly language for the experienced user. In addition, menu-driven query may be provided for the occasional user.

10. *Availability of usual data base-management features*: They include help, backup, recovery, data dictionary, data integrity, recoverability, and multiple-level data security.

11. *Statistical analysis of data*: Includes

    Standard features such as regression, correlation, time series, and regression

    Special statistical features Ease of use

    Usability for all data elements stored

12. *Reporting and analytical capabilities.* Include

    Ease of use

    On-line and batch

    Use of high-level languages

    Multiple functions

    Access over several fields

    Default formatting

    Easily understandable display graphics

    Screen display or hard copy

    Screen-development system

    Screen-zooming

13. *Interface for modelling*: Actual and historical performance data should serve as input for models. This criterion evaluates whether special interfaces and/or even a special model data base are supported.

14. *Interface for tuning of systems, communication software and applications*: Support of tuning with database segments at the most detailed level.

15. *Documentation*: Include, the actuality and update of the documentation.

16. *Implementation*: Includes the training and support prior to, during, and after implementation oil behalf of the vendor.

The decision-making procedure for the customer may be substantially facilitated when criteria are defined and the known approaches are evaluated. The principal focus of this segment is on surveying data base concepts provided by various vendors. It is very difficult to issue general-purpose recommendation for selection due to

— Different targets of network management data files and bases

— Incompatibility of different information sources

— Managebility of data files and bases

— Correlation of information amount and installation size

— Using sidestream or mainstream concepts or a combination of both.

The majority of mainframe manufactures provide performance-measurement tools and concepts, but there are only a few that also provide database for the performance management area.

Service-Level Reporter (SLR) is an IBM program product that provides information to help manage an installation. Information is collected in a data base and presented in a readily understandable format.

Graphics and colour via GDDM/PGF can be used to present information, thereby giving a versatile, easily used, pictorial display capability for use by professionals at all levels.

An SLR objective is to minimize the number of printed reports presented to management by presenting the right information in the right format and by supplementing printed reports with on-line inquiries to the SLR data base when necessary. Multiple tables can be combined in composite reports using the "view" technique.

The current Communication Network Management (CNM) offerings from IBM such as NETVIEW, NCCF, NPDA, TARA, VNCA, NLDM are primarily on-line oriented instruments. They are used mostly by network operational control for problem determination and resolution. They are in essence technical aids for facilitating the work of the network operator. None of these products provide traditional trend-reporting features. In particular, there are two areas where trend contributions are essential:

— Error and event histories

— Availability of network resources

The objective is to provide an interface between SLR and key products mentioned previously. At least for NPDA and NLDM, there are alternatives available and implemented by means of customer-defined SMF record type and customer-defined SLR log tables, summary tables, and reports, using the Adaptable log layout (ALL) feature. The principal prerequisites are the following:

— Time stamps should match the format supported by SLR.

— Only fixed format records can be selected for collection into SLR.

There are two possible ways to obtain data from NPDA and NLDM for use by SLR:

1) The data bases should be copied into a sequential file. This technique is easy to implement, but there are two basic problems:
   - Due to the wrap-count technique, records could be deleted between periodic SLR-COLLECT runs.
   - On the other hand, duplicated records can enter the SLR database when the previous ones are still in the daily NPDA NLDM data base.
2) Selected records could be written to a log file from a logging program external to NPDA and NLDM by means of an NCCF exit. Thus, COLLECT receives the data into SLR from the SMF log. This alternative is preferred by IBM because it offers the following major benefits:
   - There are no duplicate records.
   - SMF is well known and widely used.
   - All required procedures are available.
   - SLR call process all data including the CNM source-in a single collect run, saving time and resources.

At the present time, the following record types are supported for the SMF record type 131:

- NPDA. Type 08 records are event records. The subtypes 11 and 13 contain the RECFMS type 00 information, which is the source of tire event type and major and minor cause codes. Type 17 records are the statistical records. The subtypes 13 and 14 contain file detailed statistical records from the network. Primarily, traffic overview, device error, problem history reports, and the problem-determination trend can be generated. Optionally, LPDA source information can be included as well.

— NLDM. The TIM (time-ordered data) record is supported. The TIM record holds the session start and end times and the session name and resources. Primarily, resource usage and availability reports can be generated.

SLR is certainly a very useful tool with numerous benefits. The opponents of this product claim, however, that there is excessive resource demand and lack of flexibility toward querying the base and changing parameters for collecting storing and reporting. Through interactive, on-line support of data-processing systems or networks, tile Info/System Program Product enables one to collect, update, retrieve, display, and report on data-processing information with the goal of the user. Installations can use Info/System to track and review problems, to plan and coordinate changes, to maintain an inventory of all system and network resources, and to access directly current information on MVS- and network-related subjects.

For the complex networking environment, the following features are of primary importance:

— Via the profile facility, the settings for function keys, the position of the command line, and the standard output destinations for the reports can easily be determined

— Providing special interface features for the less technically competent customers, such as help desk Personnel, bank tellers, insurance clerks, airline personnel, and supermarket checkout operators can be accomplished.

— Supporting help-desk activities in recording problems quickly, simply, and efficiently anti tailoring data-entry panels to the actual need of the installation are possible.

Info/System is expected to be further developed for statistical and graphic processing. Presently, both SAS/GRAPH and GDDM/PGF can be used comfortably for reporting. The data collected by the various extractors (e.g., CMF, MONITOR, IMF, CONTROL/CICS) and performance monitors is stored and accessed via a full-function CODASYL Data Base Management System, the CMF/PDB. This DBMS facility offers database maintenance functions such as backup/ rccovery, load/update, archival, and compress/summarization. In addition, the CMF/PDB features a flexible data-manipulation language, an on-line inquiry capability, a data dictionary, and a hatch-report writer. CMF/PDB is valuable, in particular for capacity- planning-oriented acclivities. The network analyst and tuner may not find the compression degree of stored information detailed enough. Special-purpose measurement sessions, however, using any of the tools indicated, may help to overcome this problem.

The role of operations in network management is critical to the functional integrity of communication networks. The quantity and geographical distribution of network devices makes this role a most difficult one. Network management must deal with a large amount of information within a very short time interval. Without implementing a powerful network-management-oriented data base, the most important activities of network management cannot be accomplished. Thus, the majority of network monitor vendors provide a data base that could also be considered as a nucleus of general-purpose network management data bases. The usual sidestream stand-alone approach includes the following characteristics:

- Maintain current and historical data on network performance.
- Create record per network element (line group, line, control unit, and terminal) per hour.
- For each element, record the following values:
  - Number of transactions
  - Response time
  - Polling latency time
  - Line-in time
  - CPU turnaround time
  - Line-out time
  - Messages in
  - Messages out
  - Errors (NAKS)
- Update automatically once per hour.
- Provide today, yesterday, month-to-date, and year-to-date information.
- Inquiring capability using graphic displays.
- Provide statistical and exception reports.

In case of application switching for a physical address, the memory requirements can become considerable. In order not to increase product prices, the vendors are usually not interested in augmenting the database size for accommodating administration-related information. Using the NPMS 3729 network monitor, the vendor suggests the mainstream approach. The monitor provides records on all message detail, line statistics, and alarm conditions to the host system to be stored in a VSAM file for later processing. This approach is very promising, as correlation capabilities can be significantly improved.

Mainframe vendors are frequently accused of not offering user-friendly interfaces. Thus, many users are not able to properly interpret measurement results provided by mainframe vendor tools. Good examples are: RFM, GTF, NPM, and, in particular, the NCCF product family for the IBM environment. There is a limited marketplace for smaller companies to bridge the gap and provide interfaces for easily interpreted measurement results. The range of products available may be very confusing for the customer.

Starting with inexpensive, easy-to-use tools for improving readability, such as NETMAN, the far end of products provides a turnkey performance database, such as MICS. In order to bridge gaps in network-management software provided by manufacturers, independent vendors offer special-purpose solutions. These packages cover special areas of network management only but are valuable in offering short-range solutions.

NETMAN is one of these products. NETMAN collects, revises, and inquires about the operational and relational characteristics of all physical hardware and software components in the data-processing-data-communications environment. It is an on-line management tool for data network management. It maintains complete information (configuration, financial, and problem) in a single data base. The data base covers the principal activities for the network administrator. NETMAN could serve as the nucleus of a comprehensive performance data base; however, efforts for extensions must not be underestimated.

UCC-8 is a typical net work-administration support system using the principle of event management. Through on-line, integrated functions, the majority of network management problems can be solved. Virtually all events can be recorded, tracked, arid managed. Typical uses include

— Problem management. Tracking problems from initial discovery through final resolution.

— Customer-service response. Coordinating support for data-processing customers to ensure timely response and good-quality service.

— Inventory control. Managing all components of physical inventories (hardware, software, furniture, etc.) to facilitate rapid problem resolution and coordinate maintenance efforts.

— Project management. Monitoring planned changes to ensure orderly completion of all tasks.

All types of events and the actions they trigger are drawn together within a single system. Integrated functions and shared data give a complete picture of each event and its impact. Managers have available the information needed to plan, direct, coordinate, analyse, and control the activities that contribute to the success of operating and administering the communication network. UCC EIGHT is operational under CICS/VS or any OS, OS/VS, or MVS operating system. Whatever the size of the network, UCC EIGHT provides valuable assistance to all functional groups. Existing procedures for problem management, customer-service response, inventory control, and project management will be enhanced and made easier through UCC EIGHT.

Paper forms and manual logs can be replaced by on-line tracking facilities; extensive review capabilities, both on-line and off-line, give instant status of current situations and full recall of past events.Using the additional CRISS feature, the help-desk activities can be automated to a great extent. But the product is heavily administration-oriented rather than network-performance-oriented.

MIKOS provides a special purpose configuration data base for supervising deadlines, expenses, deliveries, and budgets for network-related inventory items. PNMS III is capable of addressing problem, information, inventory and configuration management. Not only the networking, but the data processing environment may also be covered. Special emphasis is on problem management, including opening, updating, and closing a problem.

At first, problems should be categorised. Information collection during opening and updating problems is by categories. After opening problems, responsibility groups track the problems to ensure rapid solution.

Alert intervals are expected to be defined by the customer. The definitions usually correspond with the categories. Alert—at multiple stages-notify management and assignment groups of failure to meet problem resolution deadlines.

The Statistical Analysis System (SAS) is a system for retrieving and managing data, performing statistical analyses, and writing reports. It includes an extensive collection of useful statistical procedures and can be used both in batch and interactively under TSO. SAS uses English-like statements, minimizes working with JCL, and provides explicit error messages, making it easily understood and used by nonprogrammers as well as programmers. SAS can be widely used, and there are overwhelming benefits in the computer-performance-evaluation area. SAS is the first tool for integrating performance-related information for further statistical processing and selective reporting. There are no limits on the data sources of SAS. Using SAS/GRAPH, all requirements of powerful reporting can be satisfied. There are standard solutions for the analysis of SMF/RMF data with SAS.

Special purpose analysis should be programmed and evaluated by the customer. However, the human resources manpower required for this effort is frequently significantly underestimated. Almost all vendors now provide interfaces for SAS. Using the version for personal computers, decentral autark processing can be accomplished well. In such cases, the centrally located SAS database segments are down-loaded for further processing. But the authorization for updates by the personal computer's owners has not yet been clarified.

MICS is an installation-management data base and reporting system for users of the IBM MVS operating system. MICS provides a database system to integrate data from an array of MVS and SNA measurement sources and comprehensive database reporting and inquiry facilities. The data base is the information foundation of MICS. It is physically organised using the SAS database management facilities and consists of a related network of small, segmented SAS files providing standard physical access to selected portions of the stored data, as well as the ability for relational data retrieval. The MICS data base is organized along a four-level structure that permits historical data analysis and presentation. Standard reporting includes the generation of management-objective reports for principal information areas such as batch, MVS-Global, TSO, IMS, availability, CICS, and networks and exception reports used as diagnostic filter to report specific problems or potential problems in diverse information areas. Despite the announcements, generating new MICS elements for additional information sources is very cumbersome and needs both human and computing resources.

A few of the system modules should be modified as well. Thus, the maintainability of all systems is becoming heavily vendor-dependent. MICS customers report the following additional experiences:

— There is a substantial additional effort for customising report required

— Excessive resource demand in terms of storage and processing

— Excellent integration capabilities

— Good interfaces to accounting and modelling

— Necessity of careful consideration of updating and archiving procedures

All vendors consider some form of summarizing data in data bases, Candle markets the OMEGAMON product family for operational control in IMS, CICS, and MVS and for degradation analysis. But until now, no data has been saved for further performance analysis and capacity planning. Recently, the company announced the availability of a performance data base (EPILOG) in tile near future. BGS is the manufacturer of the BEST/I family of modelling tools. For improving the customer interface, BGS designed and implemented special purpose capturing instruments called CAPTURE/MVS, CAPTURE/VM and CAPTURE/SNA. But these tools provide the required window into the MVS and SNA data for the capacity planner only. INFO-BASE is it database system for capacity planning and management; it enables storing, retrieving, and manipulating highly analysed information about the system's performance.

INFO-BASE interfaces with capacity-planning products such as CAPTURE/MVS and CAPTURE/VM. These products collect, analyse, and process performance data from standard data-extraction instruments such as SMF, RMF, and VMON. The database system interfaces with application-related projection (CRYSTAL) and with models for MVS and VM. The models perform what-if analysis to evaluate and to predict future performance levels. The data base is written in SAS and is hierarchical and relational at the same time. INFOBASE performs four principal operations:

— Populating tile data base from data extraction instruments.

— Maintaining the data base using a comprehensive set of procedure for aggregating, archiving, and deleting detail-level data.

— Writing reports and generating graphs.

— Generating baseline models for the MVS and VM environment.

At present, INFO-BASE supports up to five data sets for every interval. They are: SYSTEM, DEVTOT, LPATHS, WKLOAD, and DEVDET. Additional components for supporting IMS-, CICS-, and SNA-related data are under development.

The decision making in selecting the right solution for the larger organization is not easy. The following procedure may help in facilitating the selection process.

1. Preselect the products by considering installation-dependent constraints such as

   Mainframe manufacturer

   Operating system

Vendor products installed

Monitors (software, hardware, and/or network, already installed, etc.)

2. Group the criteria toward powerful performance data bases.
3. Determine the weights of criteria groups and the weights within each group, respectively, by means of a preference matrix.
4. Evaluate each product considered against all criteria and subcriteria, scoring between 0 (low) and 10 (high); or if desired, use a more flexible upper limit.
5. Compute the final results, considering weight and scores.
6. Evaluate the costs, analyse the sensitivity of results achieved in (5), and make the decision.

The general experiences using network-management-related data bases can be summarized as follows:

— The mainframe manufacturers offer only a limited scope of database capabilities, frequently biased toward a certain group of performance data.

— In many installations, the mainframe and performance tools installed significantly limit the decision-making procedure.

— There are just a few practical examples of integrating performance-related and administration-related information into a common data base.

— There are no records on the resource demand of isolated files, report generation, and redundancy when dealing with collecting, storing, and evaluating performance-related data.

— Monitor vendors suggest only special-purpose performance database concepts. In a few cases, these data bases can become the nucleus of general-purpose network-management data bases.
— Network-management and performance-oriented data are not yet sufficiently considered as basis for successful network management.
— Many customers find it difficult to justify the cost of general-purpose database concepts.
— The future will very likely dictate the implementation of independent concepts offering interfaces for almost all kinds of information resources.

Structured Query Language (SQL) is a widely accepted industry standard for defining, changing, and managing data and controlling how changes to the database are made by using tables, indexes, keys, rows, and columns to store data. Relational theory was a wide open field and that once people knew about relational theory, they would put it in a category with mathematics and accounting. IBM announced that its primary and probably only database system was to be IMS, which is a nonrelational database. Even with the release of IMS, customers demanded easier ways to retrieve data than what the database could offer. They wanted better tools and the elimination of the obstacles that made it difficult for the average person to store and retrieve data. They wanted to be able to query a database in human-like language and the ability to redefine data relationships immediately rather than once every two weeks or whenever one could assemble a team of programmers. They wanted to simplify the process required to make data definition changes to the structure holding the data and, even more than that, to access the data without being forced to use the views defined when the database was originally built or updated. The obstacles to accessing data in the non-relational environment are many.

In a network hierarchical database, a person could not add a field to a file, change the length or datatype of the field, or delete the field because the physical structure that was originally designed to store the data had to remain unchanged. Changes to the structure were brought to database change meetings and the changes were made in batches. This created a development bottleneck. Another obstacle in non-relational databases is the inability of a network or hierarchical database to query data in a freestyle manner outside of the views of the logical structure that was originally defined.

It's no wonder that programmers and customers involved in this time- consuming and expensive process began to think about the budding technology concepts of the relational databases. The relational database overcomes many obstacles to accessing the data and offers the programmer a painless alternative. A one-line command, as easy as alter table, can change the structure. There is no unload, no reload, and the data is not disturbed at all (unloading being the act of separating the actual data from the database structure). Adjustments are easily made, and all the data elements in the database can be queried flexibly. Views of the data do not have to be predefined, and relationships can be built on a moment's notice. By the mid-1970s it was recognised that relational databases were better suited to deliver the functionality the customers wanted.

In order to deal with customer demand, IBM resurrected its System R project, and relational databases began to appear in the marketplace in the early 1980s. From these early relational beginnings came Microsoft SQL Server. Microsoft originally licensed the basic building blocks of SQL Server from Sybase and made the product available on PC platforms running OS/2 and, more recently, Windows NT.

A joint effort between Sybase, Ashton-Tate, and Microsoft in 1988 produced one of the first databases on the personal computer, making the relational database more openly accessible to end users. Microsoft spearheaded the SQL Server project; AshtonTate withdrew when SQL Server was ported to the NT operating system from OS/2. Both Microsoft and Sybase sold the database on the PC hardware platform until version 4.21, but the Microsoft/Sybase partnership dissolved in 1993.

Sybase has since been concentrating on the minicomputer platform and Microsoft on the personal computer platform. In the latest release SQL Server 7, Microsoft has taken the core technology of the SQL Server database and redesigned it with more data warehouse functionality, a better optimiser, and a rewrite of the database storage engine. Also important is its improved scalability, an ongoing Microsoft focus.

Microsoft SQL Server can now store a terabyte, one thousand gigabytes, in each database. The Microsoft Enterprise concept is intent on meeting the needs of the high-end database market in the distributed computing environment and supplies all the tools to manage the many servers required in this type of computing environment, including the ability to access up to eight CPUs.

The Microsoft Management Console (MMC) is where this all comes together. The snap in functionality of the MMC allows the insertion of third-party tools to manage the environment and comes with all of the functionality of the Enterprise Manager which it houses. The method of storing data is completely different in Microsoft SQL Server version 7 than it was in version 6.5. Instead of the device paradigm for storage that allows multiple databases per physical file, we now see databases stored as files with one database per-file or group of files. In the past, the device moniker hid what was actually happening, which was the creation of an operating system file.

Now a single database can reside in multiple files via the file group feature, though multiple databases will no longer exist together in a single file. This creates a dramatic improvement in performance and capacity. It also eases the initial burden of comprehension for a new user by simplifying the concepts and taking out the confusing references to devices and the extra steps involved in creating them. The create database command now specifies the name and size of the data and log files associated with the database; the disk init statement that was used in previous versions to create the actual physical database file and the requirement to reference size in terms of the number of 2K datapages is no longer necessary (SQL Server 7 now uses 8K datapages).

Now the database size reference is in terms that most users are familiar with: kilobytes, megabytes, and gigabytes. In addition to these changes in the storage structure, there are new disk formats for rows, extents, data files, and log files. These new formats will allow the desired scalability from low-end to high-end systems while improving performance.

In an effort to improve space utilisation and image data can now be shared by multiple rows. In previous versions, if a column contained a few bytes of text or image data it would take up an entire 2K page. Now free space on the new 8K page will be used by data belonging to other rows. There is also the provision of automatic database creation and alteration when a database is restored. Just the act of issuing a command to restore a database file will automatically create and/or alter the database. This way the database administrator won't have to figure out the size of the receiving database and then create it before restoration. This is merely one example of how SQL Server 7 is much easier to administer.The combination of Microsoft SQL Server and Microsoft Internet Information Server provides the framework to connect the relational database to the internet while using web browsers to display data. This is the beginning of the era of database end-user accessibility and was not possible before internet visual browser technology, matured.

There are untold advantages of integrating the NT operating system with all of the NT Inter/intranet capabilities and the SQL Server database—by using the ODBC connectivity built into the NT operating system, Microsoft SQL Server and the NT internet information server database developers have the functionality to deliver interactive, online database content to the masses via an internet website. There is also improved support for distributed transactions and enhanced distributed management tools that allows for, seamless replication and multiple platform implementations. Total embrace of the internet technology has made this possible in ways that were unimaginable just a few short years ago.

Databases can now be replicated, via the internet and make data accessible to users in remote locations throughout the world. The improved image data type will help add rich content for the internet user.The Microsoft Exchange Server can be used with the SQL Mail part of Microsoft SQL Server and the Microsoft BackOffice product line to build intranet solutions. Intranet is similar to the internet, but the number of users is usually limited to employees within a corporation. Intranet is also protected by a firewall. With an intranet, a company, can keep its data confidential yet still have the benefits of the web environment.

Companies can use an intranet to distribute information or collect information from their employees. Many companies are moving their internal applications to intranet and lever aging them once they are there. Think of entering the hours you work on intranet or entering your expense reimbursement data into an intranet webpage which makes its way to a SQL Server, database.

Find out what the next department is doing by visiting their webpage on, intranet. The possibilities are endless, especially as they incorporate the data stored in the corporate database onto the webpage. An intranet can also be used as a proving ground for applications before them to the internet. Reliability, quick response time, and security are good reasons to embrace intranet technology. Intranets are relatively immature now, but they are moving forward as the internal communication needs of companies grow.

Businesses will not be competitive into the next century if they do not embrace the internet and intranet technologies. SQL Server 7 supports this philosophy by committing to a set of tools designed explicitly for this purpose. If data can be stored on a SQL Server 7 database, it can quickly be presented via browser technology. Scalability, the ability to add more hardware when the size of the data and the demand in number of users increases, has been a customer demand for many years. A distributed computing platform requires that this work well but, unfortunately, personal computer hardware has not stepped up to the task of distributed computing until recently. Now, however, the PC hardware comes with differing processing capabilities and multiple CPUs, and it is up to the software to harness this newly acquired power. Microsoft SQL Server is accomplishing this with the parallel execution of a single query across multiple CPUs. The interesting part of this is that Microsoft SQL Server 7 is the only database designed to run in a distributed computing environment and can, take advantage of many of the opportunities inherent in the PC platform in a way that other relational databases cannot.

The client/server model as we know it is two-tiered, which means two computers are involved, a client and a server. This does not fit well into, the scalability equation when the servers are dealing with thousands of users, so the idea of a three-tiered or multi- tiered application has come into being to meet the physical challenges of the hardware. Multi-tiered means the insertion of another computer into the mix which, for example, can implement the, business rules of the Enterprise and transform data. Microsoft Transaction Server is an associated technology that keeps the developers from having to deal with connectivity and related issues.

It is a complete two-tiered server environment for ActiveX and has automatic thread and process management and a database connection pool. The developer does not have to worry about beginning and ending transactions: if a component is flagged as transactional, the Microsoft Transaction Server creates a transaction around the processing, and those components referenced will also be included in the transaction. The product protects the developer from system-level tasks like thread management and is best used with DCOM. DCOM, sometimes referred to as COM+ is an extension to COM (Component Object Model), which will be used to build the next-generation applications for the distributed environment.

A client gets access to one of the DCOM objects and calls routines through that pointer as if the object were running on the client. DCOM has a data-binding feature that binds object and database fields. A COM server can create object instances of many object classes, and a COM object can have multiple interfaces, each representing a different way the object acts. The use of DCOM objects has been accelerated by the use of COM objects, and other related technologies, and this architecture is the basis for the technology of the future on the web for databases.

The NT Server Enterprise Edition will have Microsoft Transaction Server (MTS) and Message Queue Server built in. SQL Server Enterprise Edition uses cluster server, scalable to 16 nodes. SQL Server 7 has, 64-bit addressing to support applications that need more than the 2GB of memory allowed by 32-bit software. Windows NT and SQL Server will scale to eight processors out of the box and can use up to 3GB of application memory.

In a future unspecified release of SQL server, the database will implement massive parallelism on lop clusters, server and the components that facilitate the distributed computing environment. Also included in this mix is BackOffice Server 4.0 Enterprise Edition. It will include the enterprise versions of NT, SQL Server, Exchange, and Site Server Enterprise Edition, which includes, Commerce Server.

In addition, Wolfpack APIs allow third parties to integrate their clustering products with the Microsoft technology. This is a strategy that allows third-party products to build on the Microsoft technology. Win32 and OLE, part of the Component Object Model, are also part of the strategy and are being offered for licensing to third parties on other, operating systems. The ultimate intent of the strategy is to move from the desktop to the Enterprise. The server model is the predominant feature in the release of Microsoft software products. BackOffice has SQL Server, System, Management Server, SNA Server, MS Mail Server, and Windows NT. Windows, Component Object Model, and OLE rood out the Enterprise picture. What OLE adds is a programming model which is based on object-oriented interfaces and is defined using Microsoft, Interface Definition Language (MIDL).

OLE provides a consistent programming model across all components and objects and implements Microsoft's COM, Microsoft will begin to provide OLE interfaces for developers to use rather than APIs. The objects can be incorporated in applications using their OLE interfaces, the idea being to reuse the COM objects. Microsoft's programming interface is the Win32 API, and this interface is the central part of the strategy.

The goal is to make Win32 available on other operating systems in the form of link libraries that will allow programmers to link applications. The Win32 API has a pre-emptive scheduler for multi-tasting multi-threading, 32-bit linear memory-addressing protected memory, symmetric multi-processing capability and other features. An introduction to SQL Server 7 is not complete without mentioning clustering capabilities Clustering through the use of Microsoft's Cluster Server API will constitute a major part of the Enterprise equation by linking servers together to provide application load balancing.

When one database server fails, clustering moves them to another server, making the database a virtual database on a shared dish. Cluster Server gets services back on-fine in case of failure and helps system administrators keep systems available during maintenance procedures. The system administrator can wait for a slow time and initiate the fad-over to do maintenance on the servers.

A fail-over is when the secondary server monitoring the primary gets no response after two tries and the secondary server maintains a lock on the shared drive array with no complaint from the other server.

When that happens, the Cluster Server can move services back to the restored primary server. Cluster Server watches critical services and applications, and any protected programme that becomes unavailable is restarted on the same machine or a different server. To deal with hardware failure, Cluster Server uses one server to monitor the other. The NT Server Enterprise, will have built in transaction processing and clustering. Microsoft SQL Server and the Microsoft Transaction Server MTS will create an Enterprise software solution. The Cluster Server servers are currently linked via the SCSI bus, and both servers share an array of drives and monitor each other.

Making data available for sharing by multiple users, who sit across varied regional and national boundaries on different platforms via networked computers, is the next major phase of corporate computing, bringing about a mind-boggling growth of information through transfer tools such as the internet and intranets. But this is not easy.

For, it is virtually impossible to manage mountains of data that accumulate on innumerable different systems. Evidently, this huge accumulation of data underscores the need for a single storage box that will allow all the information to be viewed. This leads to the concept of data warehousing. The concept of maintaining a warehouse for simply dumping information in one key domain has somewhat changed today.

Whatever the IT strategy employed, companies have come to realise that any data useful for the organisational process and ERP (enterprise resource planning) systems is a corporate asset. For, data warehousing is part of the IT infrastructure that translates an asset into a competitive advantage.The concept of data warehousing, which dates back to the mid-80s, was initially intended to provide an architectural model for the flow of data from operational systems to decision-support environments.

In the absence of such an architecture, there usually existed an enormous amount of redundancy in the delivery of management information. The process of gathering, cleaning, and integrating data from various sources often resulted in replication of the data for each project. Moreover, legacy systems were frequently being revisited as new requirements emerged, each requiring a subtly different view of the legacy data.

Based on analogies with real-life warehouses, data warehouses were intended as a large-scale storehouse for distributing legacy data to retail stores, regional sales offices, or joint business partners. These were tailored for access by decision-support users. The data warehouses were designed to manage the bulk supply of data from their suppliers (i.e., operational systems). This enabled retail stores to focus on packaging, shipping, and presenting selections of the data to the end-users, rather than maintaining it.

Somewhere along the way, this analogy and architectural vision was lost and in the 80s—as software tools began to emerge with the focus on designing decision-support database analysing tools—suddenly data warehouse became the miracle cure for the decision-support headache, and suppliers jostled for a position in the burgeoning data warehousing marketplace.The critical issue facing most big enterprises today is making effective use of large volumes of data.

Data warehousing enables organisations to properly organise and manage their data for making decisions better and faster. A strong data management plays a significant role in determining competitiveness in the global marketplace. It helps devise improved methodologies for guiding resource, and is a key component in reducing risks of failure. Typically, a data warehouse is a decision-support system which integrates at a single place a plethora of diverse data and record formats, stored in a range of different systems and platforms.

This implies standardisation of data from a variety of sources to make it more easy to comprehend and apply. Executives need fast and reliable feedback about how the business is performing vis-a-vis plans, to measure success and adjust corporate strategy. Business intelligence begins with a top-down view of the key performance indicators or KPIs.

The standard queries and reports that create the KPIs may include revenue and profit growth, quality of products and services, and customer satisfaction. The data warehouse provides a quick review of these broad measures and trends, along with departures from the expected results. This allows timely executive intervention to manage the digressions from the plan. The development of a storage system to handle the growth of data is a major challenge in itself.

Implementing data warehousing is an even bigger challenge. As the practice of sharing enormous amounts of information with customers and suppliers through data warehouses is gaining prevalence, a data warehouse or business intelligence application now requires a wide range of client interfaces and the ability to both query and analyse data interactively from a variety of different client platforms. Managing a data warehouse successfully means optimising the data-storage space to ensure rapid delivery of the required information. It is also important to provide the users the right format, to access information in a manner that permits drill-down and analysis across segments, such as a product-wise and region-wise review of sales.

A successful data warehouse attracts more users and more data, thus requiring the availability of a more robust and scalable service. To ensure rapid response time, the data storage has to be simplified and automated, based on the initial and usage-based data warehouse information.

As new data sources are added, the old ones need to be changed. This is how a data warehouse evolves. Managers are bewildered as data warehousing tools and techniques proliferate with consensus neither on the best way to utilise this technology, nor on how to prepare for the future. For an IT manager, it is crucial to select a platform that provides integrated, easy-to-use tools for query, data analysis, and assessment from a wide variety of tools.

Data warehousing is heralded as the solution to the management of information impasse, and a defence mechanism against trenchant competition. It has become one of the most used and abused terms in the IT vocabulary. But ask a variety of IT solution providers and vendors for their version of what a data warehouse is and how it should be built, and the ambiguity of the term quickly becomes apparent. To most IT solution providers, a data warehouse is virtually any large database, typically in the giga-byte to the tetra-byte range, containing data from more than one source, collected for the purpose of providing management information and maintaining long-term, online storage. Some vendors of online analytical processing tools (OLAP), which gives the user the capability to perform multidimensional analysis of data, take the interpretation of a data warehouse a little further and define it as any collection of summarised data from various sources, structured and optimised for query-access.

2

Network Management

While academic libraries and many public libraries are accessible via the Internet, many resources such as private special libraries in major corporations are not as yet able to offer their catalogs in a searchable state across the Internet. With the development of what was first proposed as the National Research Education Network (NREN) and now is popularly called the "information superhighway," commercial nodes should increase and more small public libraries will be brought into this loop.

Meanwhile, individual citizens are also eager for Internet access. The Cleveland FreeNet, a member of the National Public Telecomputing Network (NPTN), offers public access to some Internet resources. Commercial suppliers such as The Well, CompuServe and Delphi and regional networks offer accounts for fees that average $30 per month for basic access. The typical university library has access to both host-based resources and distributed computing sites via typical desktop computers or more powerful UNIX-based workstations. This composite of application support reaches beyond the capabilities of any single integrated library system itself.

The decade of the nineties has produced further fine tuning of these automated library systems, with increased emphasis on workstation-based distributed applications, i.e., client/server designs, and interconnectivity and interoperability of these systems through worldwide internetworking. First, let us examine the Internet. The term "Internet" (CAPITALIZED) denotes the collection of networks that has evolved out of the Advanced Research Projects Agency (ARPA). This ARPA network uses the Transmission Control Protocol (TCP) and Internet Protocol (IP) for its architectural basis. The term "internet" (lower case) means any collection of networks that uses the TCP/IP protocol suite and is based on the Open Systems Interconnection (OSI) Reference Model.

The present Internet began with the establishment of the ARPAnet, an experimental wide area network which connected host computers and terminal servers together. The networks pioneered the concept of a layered network architecture designed to simplify design, implementation and operation of large networks of diverse computing equipment.

A specialized network called the NSFnet, operated by the National Science Foundation to link supercomputer sites, eventually assumed the ARPAnet traffic. Currently, the Internet encompasses over 2,218 distinct networks, according to the tables kept at the DDN Network Information Center.

The Informational Sciences Institute (ISI) does much of the research, standardization and allocation work of the Internet. Information services for the Internet are provided largely by SRI, International. Each independent network connected to the Internet has its own operations center. For example, the ARPAnet was operated by BBN, under contract from DARPA.

All of these interconnected networks use the TCP/IP protocols and incorporate layered architectures based on the OSI Reference Model. Every major research network worldwide now has some sort of connection to the Internet. Accessing these resources for basic service requires use of three pieces of software on your microcomputer or host system. These are Telnet, TN3270 and FTP.

Telnet software, allows a host-connected terminal or microcomputer on a LAN to emulate a Digital Equipment Corp. VT100 family terminal, or in some cases another emulation, in order to log on to another network-attached computer. The TN3270 program provides similar services, except that the emulation is for IBM computers using the IBM 3270 emulation for IBM 3178/3278 terminal models.

FTP is a program that implements the file transfer protocol, which allows a user to send or receive ASCII or binary-type files to or from a remote host, using commands that are relatively host independent and that support locating the appropriate file source or destination. Further services require Gopher client software to access these numerous Gopher information servers.

Similarly, the World Wide Web (WWW), which uses Hypertext to provide information, requires a client such as Mosaic or Cello for Windows 3.1. Gopher servers worldwide are indexed through a service called Veronica.

Similarly, Archie servers index major anonymous FTP file repositories on the Internet. WAIS is another locational service to find various Internet accessible resources. Gopher servers often provide a connection to these search servers, or they may be accessed directly.

The internal network workings are defined in a set of documents called Request for Comments (RFCs). If you have an issue to bring before the Internet, you can write it up as an RFC, to be considered for formalization. Jon Postel is the RFC referee to whom any proposal is sent. He will electronically broadcast the RFC for comment by anyone who wishes to use Internet electronic mail. These RFCs can be classified into five groups: required, suggested, directional, informational and obsolete. An example of a required RFC would be RFC-791, which defines the Internet Protocol (IP).

Because it is required, it must be implemented on every connected host computer. Suggested RFCs such as RFC-793, Transmission Control Protocol, are generally implemented by network hosts, since they do impact on useability. Directional RFCs are ones that have been discussed and agreed upon but not widely applied. An example is RFC-937, the Post Office Protocol, which was not felt to be widely needed. However, if a site feels certain protocols are needed, then they should implement them according to the agreed upon RFC.

Informational RFCs contain factual information about the Internet and its operation. For example RFC-990 tells how numbers are assigned for the numeric IP addresses for each host on the Internet. The last category, obsolete RFCs, is needed because RFCs which supersede earlier ones may not be completely understandable by themselves as they may not include the whole model, only the changes and their rationale.

Another part of the Internet that users should know is the Network Information Center (NIC). The facility is available to all Internet users. Network and telephone may be used to contact the NIC, with the most prevalent contact being electronic mail on the network. This is done by using the Telnet software facility to access nic.ddn.mil. Anonymous FTP is used to retrieve selected documents.

For IP address and domain name assignments, one must contact the NIC electronically with a message to hostmaster@nic.ddn.mil. The way most people keep up to date on network news is to subscribe to one or more mail reflectors. These are special electronic mailboxes which broadcast received messages to those subscribing addresses. The NIC provides a registration service for mail reflectors in the files netinfo: interest-groups 1 .txt; netinfo: interest-groups-2.txt; and netinfo:interest-groups3.txt. How does all of this message traffic get to the appropriate destinations? It does so by using a standard unique IP address. The path to this address is controlled by routing schemes through gateways that pass on the message between connected networks comprised by the Internet. The IP address is allocated by the NIC above via an application template by email to the above NIC address. These addresses take the form of four decimal numbers separated by periods. Each number is the value of an octet of 32 bits, e.g., 128.39.7.90.

Addresses have different meanings for these octets, depending on the net organization, i.e. one net with lots of nodes or a hierarchical site of nets with fewer nodes each. Thus, there are Class A, B and C networks. Class A networks have the first octet as a network address and the remaining three as a host address on that network. Class B networks use the first two Octets as a network address and the last two as the host address. Class C addresses use three octets as the network address and one as the host. All Class A networks have now been assigned, so that any current applications must choose Class B or C. There is an infrequently encountered Class D for multi-cast-type networks that may seen more frequently in the future. Also, for purely experimental networks, there is a Class E experimental format.

Since these IP addresses are not very easily remembered by humans, a symbolic name register was set up at the NIC where the IP address was to be equated to a text form address such as "lambda." However, with the Internet expansion, a domain-based symbolic name in the form "sun.min.stk.edu" is more commonly used by users when sending messages or accessing remote computers. The root of this tree is the rightmost group of characters. In the example above, "edu" is the domain service educational institutions, "sun" is the actual computer's name and, within the subdomain method of allocation, "min" is a subdomain within the institution "stk."

Root name servers are contacted by software on the user's machine, called a resolver, to determine who is responsible for these first-level domains. What root server to contact is an installation parameter. The resolver finds out who provides "edu" or another domain's services. Then, it contacts the "edu" or other domain name server, which supplies it with a list of addresses of servers for the subdomains, such as "stk" above. Next, the subdomain server similarly gives another portion, such as "min," until the final subdomain returns a list of addresses of interfaces on that host, e.g., "sun" in the above example. With this background on the Internet, it is time to consider the utility of the Internet to libraries as well as some resources of interest to librarians and information specialists. The early developers' conception of the Internet was of a pathway between a few supercomputer sites connecting fewer than 100 systems across the United States.

The growth of the Internet as a much wider utility really took off beginning in 1989. In just a few short years, the following benefits of Internet growth have been amply demonstrated:

— Direct search access to the major research library catalogs in the developed world, with more additions each year

— Ability of one institution to provide its clienteles access to a remote service provided by another information provider

— Access to rapidly expanding numbers of scholarly journals in electronic form and electronic archive sites for collections of these electronic publications

— Mail reflectors, or in the language of BITNET, Listserv's or Usenet's News Groups, devoted to hundreds of topics, allowing concerned communities to have continuing interactions that are rapid and dynamic compared with annual scholarly meetings, telephone conferencing or conventional mail

— Data transfer among researchers that can be accomplished in minutes or hours instead of days or weeks,

— Archive sites to serve as repositories for much public domain or shareware distributed software, accessible to Internet connected users just as microcomputer bulletin boards have made such resources available to the modem-equipped community

— Worldwide electronic mail, including gateways between such disparate commercial services as MCI Mail or CompuServe

— Ability of users to secure accounts on remote computers for specialized software or other resources, with a savings in telecommunications costs since each Internet connected site pays for the line charge to its regional network hub

Internet's functions being taken over by the National Research Education Network (NREN), following the enabling legislation Congress passed on November 22, 1991. On that date a final compromise version of the High Performance Computer Act was sent to the White House. This act is now signed and forms the basis for President Bill Clinton's initiative on the National Information Infrastructure Act of 1993, which describes further initiatives to bring about the NREN. This legislation provides funding authority for two-thirds of the NREN to the National Science Foundation and the remainder to an interagency group under the White House Office of Science Technology Policy. Internet-connected host computers provide Transmission Control Protocol (TCP) services to their users through the NCSA Telnet software. This program allows a user on one system to emulate a terminal on another system, usually a Digital Equipment Corp. VT100 family terminal, although several other emulations are sometimes encountered.

For systems that are either IBM or compatible mainframes, where IBM 3278 terminal emulation is the norm, the TN3270 software is used. Its services are similar to those of Telnet. UNIX-based computer systems provide these programs as part of the UNIX operating system facilities. Sun Computer pioneered UNIX as an operating system of choice for engineering and scientific workstations. Other competing workstation manufacturers such as Hewlett-Packard, IBM and NeXT Computer also use UNIX and provide this TCP protocol. The third piece of software used across the Internet is the File Transfer Protocol (FTP) program. This allows either sending or receiving an ASCII or binary-type file, independent of various proprietary file transfer schemes.

It also allows access to whatever directory and subdirectory structure may be present on the host computer being accessed, using a common command set that frees the user from having to know the specifics of each system. Thus, one command, "cd," for example, allows a user to change to the proper directory to either find the file desired or to receive the file the user wishes to upload. This command means "Change Directory" and can be used independent of the type or brand of host computer connected to the Internet. For the microcomputer user-either MS/PC-DOS or Macintosh-Telnet, TN3270 and FTP are available as public domain programs, usually supplied by campus computer centers but also downloadable by FTP from several Internet servers.

If such systems are connected directly to a campus or institution-based backbone network having its own IP address registered with the DDN NIC, all of the systems connected will also have their own unique address within that network and will be able to access Internet resources without any host computer intervention. These LANs can be provided a numeric IP address and their own English alphabet domain name form.

An Ethernet card is used in these microcomputers and the above software can be used in appropriate format for these systems. To complete such a connection it is also necessary to obtain the correct packet driver software for the Ethernet card. A number of these have been developed at Clarkson University and constitute the Clarkson Packet Driver distribution also available from sites distributing the NCSA Telnet software.

These Clarkson drivers have now been taken over by Crynwyr and are being distributed as the Crynwyr drivers ' Before connecting to your backbone network, be sure to cheek with your network administration as to what specific Ethernet cards perform best with your backbone and to obtain the correct Crynwyr packet driver for that card. The staff of computer centers, while they may have had some RFC's tucked away, usually had little to offer in the way of helpful descriptions or addresses of archive sites or specific resources. Also, if you did not know the electronic mail address of your recipient you could not send that party mail electronically on the Internet.

Unfortunately, this latter situation still presently holds true, although it is easier now to find out the IP address or the domain-based symbolic name for a given computer site. There are some valuable guides to various Internet resources that have been compiled, and these should become familiar to all who would use the Internet for more than electronic mail services.

For Internet beginners, Brendan P. Kehoe has produced "Zen and the Art of the Internet: A Beginner's Guide to the Internet. This is available for Anonymous file transfer from various sites, but the author can be contacted at Widener University via the Internet, using the address brendan@cs. widener.edu, The mother of Internet guides is a collection of indexes by Robert Elton Maas. As of December 23, 199 1, his indexes were in version 0. 16. The first part of this collection is called "maasinfo.topindex." It contains addressing and accessing information to 52 resources, including files available only by Internet FTP or electronic mail daemon. He does not include any files that are only available within Usenet News groups or dial-up, modem-accessed bulletin boards. Maas has built this index with contributors of resources, who receive a waiver of a shareware payment in return for their contribution.

Surprisingly, although resources in the hobby bulletin board networks like FidoNET or RBBSnet are not included, Maas is reachable for short messages over FidoNET, with the address ROBERT.MAAS@F212.N 143.ZI.FIDONET. ORG or as rem@darkside.com. Typical of entries in this index is the following entry:

> "INTEREST. GROUPS (800K) The famous "List of Lists", every known open mailing list and digest on the Internet and Bitnet, in alphabetical order. (Mail to: i interest-groups-request@ nisc. sri. com to add or delete an entry to that list.) (Bad news from nisc@nisc.sri.com (Steven, for the SRI NISC: INTEREST.GROUPS is not updated with any great frequency at this time.)
>
> To: LISTSERV@NDSUVMI
>
> GET INTEREST PACKAGE (511 K, old version?, split into eleven pieces)
>
> To: mail-server@nisc.sri.com
>
> Send netinfo/interest-groups (817K, split into 23 pieces)
>
> FTP ftp.nist.sri.com (192.33.33.22) netifo/interest-groups (80OK)
>
> FTP noc.sura.net (192.80.214. 100) nic/interest groups (800K)
>
> FTP csuvaxl.csu.murdoch.edu.au (134.115.4.1) pub/library/listof. lists (80OK)"

This entry assumes the reader knows how to send electronic mail from his or her site on the Internet and how to use the FTP software to get files. The second part to this index of indexes is maasinfo.docindex. This is a bibliography of online tutorials and other useful documents for the user to learn how to use many available Internet and BITNET resources. For example, one very useful document is the Inter-Network Mail Guide, which describes how to send electronic mail from one network to another, such as from Internet to CompuServe or MCI Mail, given that you know the local address of your recipient.

To obtain this guide written by John J. Chen, you can send the email message GET NETWORK GUIDE to LISTSERV @UNMVM. Or you may FTP to ftp.syr.edu (128.230.1.49) for networks/doc/ ingmail.txt. The third part is maasinfo.hownet. This briefly describes how to get started using various network services. The fourth part is called maasinfo. archie. It explains a file-finding database service called " Archie. "If you know the file name, "Archie" will find the FTP site. Several other smaller files complete maasinfo, such as maasinfo.mactexed, which lists shareware and public domain text editors for the Apple Macintosh computers. Another Internet resource tool is the NNSC Internet Tour, a Macintosh Hypercard stack. It is a rather general introduction but contains some valuable leads to data archive sites.

The mainly UNIX network called Usenet, which is one of the Internet connected networks, has many news groups, since this is its purpose. These are similar to the BITNET Listserv or the Echo Conference in the FidoNET electronic bulletin board network. Each of these is devoted to a specific topic and has some sort of moderator that makes sure that relevant discussions are the norm. These Usenet news groups are listed in act. news. newusen, compiled by Gene Spafford, and it can be obtained via anonymous FTP to pit-manager.mit.edu (18.72.1.58) in the directory: pub/usenet /news. announce. newusers/list of active newsgroups.

Edward Vielnetti (emv@msen. corn) has revised the Spafford list, and this is available by FTP from ftp.cs. toronto.edu (128.100.3.6) in pub/emv/news-archives/listofnews-groups. There are other lists of discussion or conferences on the Internet. For example, BITNET Listserv fists can be obtained by sending an email message to either of two different sites.

The first is to LISTSERV@DARTCNIS I, with the message SEND LISTSERV LIST, or via anonymous FTP to DARTCMS 1. DARTMOUTH.EDU. (129.170.16.19) in SIGLISTS/LISTSERV.LISTS.

The second is to LISTSERV @ NCSUVM, with the message LIST GLOBAL, or by anonymous FTP to utar 1 vml.uta.edu (129.107.1.6) in directory bitnet/listserv lists. The "Directory of Scholarly Electronic Conferences" overlaps with the previous two lists. It is compiled by Diane K. Kovacs (dkovacs@ kentvm.bitnet) and can be obtained by sending a message to LISTSERV@KENTVM @ or LISTSERV @ BROWNVM or LISTSERV @ UOTTAWA. The message to any of these sites should read:

GET ACADLIST README

GET ACADLIST INDEX

GET ACADLIST FILE1

GET ACADLIST FILE2

GET ACADLIST FILE3

GET ACADLIST FILE4

GET ACADLIST FILES 5

GET ACADLIST FILE6

Dana Noonan is the author of a shorter and more concise list of library catalogs accessible via Telnet or TN3270. This list can be obtained by anonymous FTP to hydra.uwo.ca (129.100.2.13) in directory libsoft/ internet- libraries.txt. In addition, Peter Scott is the creator of Hytelnet which is a Hypertext guide following the form of the Barron list. Peter Scott's address is aa375 @ freenet.carleton.ca. Hytelnet lists Internet and Britain's JANET-connected libraries, campus-wide information systems and other database resources.

To keep up to date, subscribe to the HYTEL-L listserv at bytel-l@kentm.kent.edu. Finally, three is Richard Duggan's CATALIST which is a Hypertext version of the Barren guide that runs under Microsoft Windows 3.1. Duggan may be reached at duggan@brahms.udel.edu. Anony-mous FTP will obtain this list from zebra. acs.udel.edu in the directory pub/library. The filenames are cat 10.exe, fullcat.exe and readme.txt. Since one of the basic activities you will want to perform on the Internet is file transfer through the FTP protocol, Jeff Linder has created "File Transfer Protocol-Basic Primer." Obtain it by sending the e-mail message GET FTP PRIMER to LISTSERV@TEMPLEVM.

These are the major resource guides to the Internet that you will want to examine. Others can be located that describe specific services or sites. There are over 800 sites on the Internet that offer anonymous file transfer and serve as servers for distributing software programs, particularly programs in the public domain. Since over one million files exist, finding these can be difficult and often rather frustrating.

McGill University programmers have created software for a server called Archie, which maintains catalogs of many of these sites and their files. It is updated monthly, so it is reasonably up to date. The best way to connect to an Archie server is by Telnet or, Gopher, although command line and X-windows clients do exist for many systems and email access can be done via FTP by mail servers such as BITFTP@PUCC for BITNET-only users. Some currently operating Archie servers are:

archie.ans.net	(New York)
archie.rutgers.edu	(New York)
archie.sura.net	(Maryland)
archie.unl.edu	(Nebraska)
archie.mcgill.ca	(Canada- first Archie site)
archie.funet.fi	(Finland)
archie.au	(Australia)
archie.doc.ic.ac.uk	(Great Britain)

Log in to an Archie site by typing "archie" and after a greeting you will see an "archie >" prompt. Enter Help as a command to receive instructions on using the "prog" command to search as well as Archie's other commands. Another feature of Archie is the Whatis database, which gives names and synopses of over 3500 public domain programms on the Internet. Another program of interest is Gopher, whose first server is available at the University of Minnesota by Telnet (V nesota resources and computer-related information and electronic books and directories of some Internet resources special to this mother Gopher server at Minnesota.

Gopher can be reached at consultant. micro.umn.edu. Log in from Telnet as "gopher." If you are coming in via an A-NET connection from an IBM host, log in as "anet." The VT100 emulation is not very good on this server when compared to the software for MS-DOS and Macintosh which is distributed by boombox. micro.umn.edu. Over a thousand Gopher servers are now operating on the Internet. Gopher clients are available for Windows 3.1 from NOTIS, Inc. (WinGopher) and as shareware from several popular FTP sites (HGOPHER v.2.4, BCGopher). VERONICA (Very Easy Rodent Oriented Net-wide Index to Computerized Archives) servers index the contents of Gopher servers. They usually limit the maximum number of items retrieved to 200 and are accessible through various Gopher servers.

Another index server is provided by WAIS (Wide Area Information Service). It searches collections of data, i.e., databases, on the Internet. Someone has to create an index for the server to use in a search. It uses a relevance score to order its search results and is not a Boolean system. To directly use WAIS, you can use a Telnet client to log into think.com or nnsc.nst.net. At the login, type "wais" to run a character-oriented interface.

There are several client programs also available from popular FTP sites. Some Gopher servers provide WAIS search connections or implement WAIS-type indexing on their Gopher server content. The World Wide Web (WWW) is a hypertext-based knowledge system with linking capabilities to other systems and resources similar to Gopher. The Hypertext pages are created with Hypertext Markup Language (HTML), and Internet resources are tied through Uniform Resource Locator (URL) addresses.

Local area networks (LANs) create a building or floor-level network connecting personal computers or workstations to shared resources provided by computers acting as servers. Also, for smaller LANs peer-to-peer networks can be set up to provide printer and program sharing. Windows for WorkGroups, Novell Lite and LANtastic are the most popular of these.

These dedicated servers on a server-based network, such as Novell 3.12, can be file servers supporting multiuser applications, special work group software or communications servers acting as gateways to remote host computers or other networks. They can also provide sharing of high quality or specialized print or other output devices and storage media such as CD-ROM or WORM units. Electronic mail systems are another obvious benefit from LANs. Multiple LANs can be interconnected for institution-wide networks that might span a metropolitan area or reach across a country or even the world.

The metropolitan area network (MAN) and wide area network (WAN) build on the local area network concept, i.e., to enable data transmission between computer users and their computing resources for rapid communication and computer-based solutions to applications that could not be approached without these facilities. Basic LAN technologies were actually conceived in the early 1960's when the earliest networks were built.

These included IBM's building of American Airlines' SABRE airline reservation network, connecting 60,000 video terminals all over the United States to six large-scale computers in 1964. However, the first real computer network was the SAGE (Semi-Automatic Ground Environment) system for the U.S. Department of Defense. It was designed in the early 1950's at the Lincoln Laboratories of the Massachusetts Institute of Technology. Ethernet is the most widely implemented LAN, with its original specification based on a coaxial cable transmission medium.

Currently, it can also be implemented using a thin coaxial-type cable called ThinNet or unshielded type 5 twisted-pair wire under the 10-BaseT specification. Today, Ethernet handles 10-Mbps transmission rates on conventional LAN media. Implemented on fiber optic cable in backbone configurations, it can support 100-Mbps transmission rates. This is the 10-BaseF protocol, which is composed of 10 Base-FP, for passive fiber, and which uses an optical splitter at the hub, and 10Base-FB, which defines Ethernet as a fiber backbone network.

These are being proposed as revised chapters of WEE 802.3, which is the Ethernet protocol standard. AT&T developed STARLAN as a LAN that can be implemented with either coaxial or twisted-pair cable. Its 1-Mbps transmission rate makes it a relatively slow LAN but one with excellent reliability. Datapoint Corp. developed ARCnet in the mid-1970's on coaxial cable media. It is the easiest to install and the least expensive to implement. It has a limit of 75 users per network and a 2.5-Mbps transmission rate. It is very reliable and is appropriate for smaller workgroup architecture. Its major drawback is its limited connectivity with bridges or gateways that are available with Ethernet or Token Ring architectures.

The last major LAN architecture is Token Ring, originally developed by IBM and now available from many other suppliers such as Proteon. It has been implemented in two variations: the original 4-Mbps and the newer 16-Mbps transmission rate. The 16-Mbps Token Ring uses IBM's premises wiring system or special type 1 shielded twisted-pair cable, while the lower speed version can be implemented on type 3 unshielded twisted-pair cable. Many Token Ring adapter cards for 16-bit bus systems are available as a 4/16 arrangement, permitting the card to be used with either speed network. Token Ring is moderately difficult to install, works best with the IBM premises wiring system and is the highest cost LAN to install. These combination 4-MB and 16-MB Token Ring cards are much more expensive than 10-BaseT cards.

The most popular physical LAN strategies are Ethernet in ThinNet and 10-BaseT versions and 4-Mbps Token Ring from IBM or competing vendors. There also are some special-purpose LANs that use wireless technology and some nonserver peer-to-peer-type networks, such as LANtastic, which allow resources on one LAN-attached computer to be shared by other LAN-attached computers. Photonic's PhotoLink is an example of an interesting wireless LAN that uses an infrared light beam to transmit and receive signals using a line-of-sight technique for the infrared light beam units. Microsoft's Windows for Workgroups v.3.11 is rapidly gaining market share in the peer-to-peer market. MANs and WANs have ben made possible by the development of fiber optic cable technology used in fiber-distributed data interchange (FDDI) backbone networks.

In these situations, different protocols may be supported such as Digital Equipment Corp. DECnet, which is based on Ethernet; OSI; TCP/IP; or Novell's IPX to link LANs into MANs and WANs. Value-added networks, such as GTE Telenet, Tymnet or Uninet in the United States and Datapac in Canada, also provide connections for WAN traffic. The development by AT&T of TI service, which is a 1.544-Mbps telephone line equal to 24 leased lines with redundancy, and its even faster T3 line transmission have made it is possible to handle relatively high speed computer-to-computer traffic.

Another advancement, which was conceived some time ago, is the Integrated Services Digital Network (ISDN) which is designed to provide telephone, data, and video signals for service providers to offer video, security, database or videotext services to an organization. ISDN is now finally taking off in the marketplace after a very slow start.

The International Standards Organization (ISO) pioneered the Open .Systems Interconnection (OSI) Reference Model, which is a description of a layered communication protocol for computer-to-computer networking. Libraries embraced this reference model very early, as the Library of Congress Linked Systems Project was implemented as closely to the reference model as the then-current hardware and software technologies and products would permit. Some deviation was necessary as some definitions had not yet been developed or accepted as standards, nor were commercial programs available for implementation at each of the layers.

With the experiences of other network architectures and with lessons learned from actual implementation of the OSI Reference Model, there will be revisions to incorporate more emphasis on internetworking, as has happened with the Department of Defense network model. An excellent collection of articles on the OSI situation is in *Library Hi-Tech* 8(4): Layer 1 is the physical interconnection level. It is implemented in the RS-232C physical serial device interface standard. Layer 2, Data Link, is specified in the Institute of Electrical and Electronics Engineers (IEEE) Standard 802 series. The ISO, under its 802 group, has accepted these WEE standards. The IEEE LAN Standards Committee 802 has approached this layer by defining logical link and medium access control, with work still being done on layer 3. ISO 802.3 defines Carrier Sense Multiple Access/Carrier Detect network protocol, which is Ethernet's scheme to prevent contention on the network. ISO ,802.4 and 802.5, respectively, define Token Bus and Token Ring techniques,, the latter used in IBM's Token Ring network. The Internet Protocol (IP) is an implementation of layer 3 of the OSI ,Reference Model while the Transmission Control Protocol (TCP) is an implementation of layer 4. These protocol were put into widespread usage with the implementation of the Sun workstation, which used UNIX as its operating system. TCP/IP was implemented in UNIX to provide networking support.

The Simple Mail Transfer Protocol (SMTP) handles layers 5 to 7 for Internet messaging. Telnet and FTP also handle layers 5 to 7. It will be quite a while before the full OSI protocol suite will replace TCP/IP on the Internet; however, current network directions indicate that eventually some modified OSI layered architecture will form the basis of many computer-to-computer networks and also be supported along with Novell's IPX and IBM's Netbios on LANs.

As Digital Equipment Corp. and IBM move to develop OSI Reference Model-compliant products within their DECnet and System Network Architecture offerings respectively, these products will also change for the better.

There are two specialized networks that have been devised. The first is the Manufacturing Automation Protocol (MAP), developed by General Motors Corp. It uses the IEEE 802.4 Token Bus standard for its lower layers and the OSI Reference Model for its upper layers. It is designed for process control and factory floor automation. The second is Technical and Office Product System (TOPS), developed by Boeing Computer Services.

It uses either WEE 802.3 or 802.5 at its lower layers and the OSI Reference Model in the upper layers. Advanced Peer-to- Peer Communications is IBM's term for its Logical Unit (LU) 6.2 service. LU 6.2 provides basic internetworking services where applications communicate as equal partners, sharing management responsibilities. Any LU 6.2-based application can initiate a session with another LU 6.2 remote partner. These partners negotiate the roles that each will assume. Low-entry networking allows this without mediation by the mainframe computer, although on older hierarchical SNA network sites, the mainframe must still mediate LU 6.2 sessions.

The IBM Document Interchange Architecture and System Network Architecture Distribution Services (SNADS) are examples of LU 6.2 applications. Today's large LANs often are an interconnection of different vendors' hardware and software, since networks grow over time, usually from a series of LANS designed to serve workgroup solutions. For example, a library may have installed a series of LANs to solve current problems.

These might be for printer sharing, access to CD-ROM or access to an integrated online library system. When the number of networks is relatively small, interconnection is relatively easy and it costs about the same to connect each additional network. In this figure, when the network can no longer be supported at a reasonable cost, the complexity barrier is reached. Beyond that point, the network would be severely constrained and unable to grow or even continue responding to users' or libraries' needs.

For these connections of disparate LANs, there are two technologies-bridging and routing-that can provide a solution based on accepted standards. Since traffic bottlenecks at the point of LAN connections are often a problem, proper utilization of these technologies can assure satisfactory performance. A bridge is a device that connects separate networks into a single logical network. A router connects separate networks into an internetwork in which each network retains its logical identity as a separate network segment.

In terms of the OSI Reference Model, a bridge operates at the data link layer 2, while a router operates at the network layer 3. If extended network length is needed in a building, it is possible to incorporate devices called "repeaters" between LAN segments. These repeaters operate at the physical layer 1 of the OSI Reference Model. Repeaters merely regenerate signals to accommodate extended wire lengths. A gateway device is essentially a protocol converter and can operate at any layer of the OSI Reference Model. Bridges work with device addresses and use these to determine what to do with data packets.

Since information about paths or routes through the network is encoded in network addresses and these are accessible only to device operating at the network layer, the bridge is a relatively simple device and therefore its cost can be kept low. Since routers operate at the network layer and know the network in both network address and path terms, they also "know" which path is the shortest or other details affecting choice of path.

Because of this, routing software is more complex than that of bridges, while the actual hardware device itself may be the same. Today, the LAN suppliers build in the functionality through the software, creating more flexibility for network designers. The OSI Reference Model and the TCP/IP protocol are both vendor-independent standards for fully interoperable internetworking. The products available in the interconnection market break down into local-and wide-area products. Devices meant for local use permit connection to local media and network backbones. These may be coaxial, twisted-pair or fiber-optic media.

Local-area devices can connect dissimilar media of two networks. Wide-area devices are equipped with two or more long-distance communications ports and at least one local port. These long-distance connections typically are leased point-to-point lines with speeds of 19.2-kbps to 2.048-Mbps capacities. How basically does a bridge work? It uses source and destination addresses to create a database. These devices "learn" on the basis of source addresses and they "forward" on the basis of the destination address. They also perform a "filtering function" if the destination address is on the same network segment as the source, the bridge automatically discards it. This prevents unnecessary traffic congestion on the bridge since only packets destined for the addresses on the other network segments pass over the bridge. If a destination address is not in the database, the bridge forwards the packet in a flooding" process, sending it to all network segments connected to its ports except the port where the source address is assigned. Once the packet is received by the correct destination, this information is then added to the database. Current router products are capable of handling multiple protocols through appropriate software. Protocols that do not contain a network layer, such as Digital Equipment Corp.

Local Area Transport terminal connection protocol, IBM's LU 6.2 and IBM's Netbios, are not able to be handled by a router. These can be passed only by a bridge or passed through another network to a network destination address capable of handling that protocol. The router database contains a "routing table" with the actual path to be used. Although some devices in environments requiring absolute security are handled by the network administrator through routing tables built into a static routing setup, the more common method is a "dynamic routing," where the router itself broadcasts information when it detects network changes. Institutions usually construct a fiber-optic FDDI type backbone having 100-200 Mbps bandwidth. This FDDI can be installed as a growth vehicle on the same fiber used in an Ethernet/ 802 fiber-optic backbone LAN.

Certainly, the future in data networking is to increase the bandwidth to accommodate heavier traffic. This implies an eventual extension of FDDI to the desktop in one scenario and might result in new LAN architectures that will extend the ISDN concept. 100-Mbps LANs will be needed to operate multiimedia LAN applications involving sound a graphics. Automated library systems benefit from more standardization, both in data processing as well as applications. With standardization, it is practical for system developers to produce products with more acceptance and broader appeal.

For the library, it also means that investments in information technology will use common and accepted parameters. This will ensure a wider choice of systems products for the future, with more preservation of hardware and software dollars already invested. For example, standards such as ISO 2709, which provides a magnetic tape record layout standard for data interchange, forms the basis for placing USMARC records onto magnetic tape, while USMARC defines the data element and logical layout of the actual bibliographic data. In a far-reaching way, other standards adopted by the National Institute of Standards and Technology (NIST) or Federal Information Processing Standards (FIPS) and those of other bodies, such as the IEEE, affect library information technologies. Now, let us examine the major player in developing American National Standards affecting library and information retrieval applications. NISO develops standards that, when adopted, become American National Standards (ANS). Its predecessor organization was known as the American National Standards Institute Subcommittee Z39 (ANSI Z39). Thus NISO's adopted standards carry the identification number Z39.xx, with the xx denoting the specific standard number.

As of January, 1994, there were 29 active and adopted standards in force. Some current standards are in the process of revision, since every five years standards must be examined for possible revision and revoked or reaffirmed if not to be revised. Three new draft standards were being balloted. Z39 standards have increasingly addressed issues that have been brought out by the use of computer and communication systems. Early standards were directed at items such as Z39.4-Basic Criteria for Indexes or Z39.5-Abbreviations of Titles of Publications. New standards are exemplified by Z39.58-Common Command Language, Z39.67-Computer Software Description. Several standards currently having a wide impact deserve specific mention here as they will affect current and future library systems. The first of these is Z39.50-Information Retrieval Application Service Definition and Protocol: Specification for Open Systems Interconnection. This is actively being implemented by major bibliographic utilities and system developers.

The sixth meeting of the Z39.50 Implementor's Group at OCLC on September 810, 1991 saw over 25 organizations attending. They have developed a list of proposed enhancements for the next version of this standard, i.e., version 3, Version 2 has been adopted and version 3 is a work in progress. ISO's Technical Committee 46 also began working on its version 3 of their corollary standard. Z39.50 is the application layer protocol by which two computers can communicate. It offers the promise of designing intelligent front-end programs that will help and mediate access by users.

Implementation of Z39.50 may be done using TCP for the immediate future since TCP is widespread, whereas full OSI support is commercially lacking. As of December 6, 1991 there were three interoperating Z39.50 implementations in test operation. These are

Pennsylvania State University (PSU) on a VAX 9000 under VMS, University of California, Division of Library Automation (UCDLA) on an IBM 3090 under MVS/ESA and the University of California, Berkeley (UCB), on a DEC system 5810 under Ultrix v.4.2.

In each case of interoperation an Init and Search cycle was completed and MARC records were returned. PSU was a server to UCDLA and UCB clients in one series. UCDAL was a server to UCB as a client and UCB was a server to a DLA client. Given the nature of this work, one thing can be assured. That is that later versions of this standard will be functionally improved since this sort of protocol technique requires staged development based on some experience.

In 1994, all the major library automation system vendors are working on Z39.50 compliant clients and many also on servers. Several vendors have released commercial production versions of their products. Also of considerable importance is Z39.58-Common Command Language. For library users and librarians, given the wide interconnection of library systems now possible, it would be nice if one set of commands could be learned and become the common basis for searching these disparate systems. Given the eventual trend toward graphical user interfaces (GUIs) as exemplified in current microcomputer software and workstation user interface shells under UNIX, it is only a matter of time that host-based library systems will also incorporate such GUI facilities, most likely adopting one of the UNIX GUIs such as X-Windows or MOTIF.

When that occurs there will need to be some GUI Standard, but most importantly, there will need to be a translation from the GUI to a common command language set if systems are to become more hardware and platform independent. Therefore, Z39.58 becomes an important cornerstone to the eventual emergence of future standards covering GUI approaches. This will assure the widest interoperability and interconnectivity on the application level for all bibliographic systems. Z39.2 defined a format for bibliographic information interchange.

However, another important thrust is being made through ANSI X12 organization electronic data interchange (EDI) work. The Data Interchange Standards "Association-linc..is the major group responsible for X12 EDI standards development, and the Book Industry Systems Advisory Committee and the Serials Industry Systems Advisory Committee are actively working with publishers, agents and library system developers to develop EDI between libraries and their material suppliers. Orders, claims, quotes and other financial and status data are all amenable to being facilitated by EDI application. Standards development is a consensus process within the various standardization bodies.

3

Online Databases

Online computer systems are usually 'real time' systems. Such a real time computer interacts with processes external to its system in real time, which means 'as they occur'. The intake data are processed on arrival at the computer system and summarised instantaneously on the display screen as output. The real time processing operation is in a parallel time relationship with the on-going activity and producing information instantaneously to be useful in controlling the current activity. Since non-perceptible time is the only factor in the real time operation, a real time operation is made in the online system. But all online operations need not be real time ones.

In the real time system, answers are instantaneously to be used in influencing the process underway. In the real time operation, parallel time relationship is essential with ongoing activities. Thus, information retrieval is instantaneous by controlling the dynamic activities. In real time processing, many remote stations may be connected directly by the high-speed communication system with the central processor, and several stations may be operating simultaneously. In modern computer system, 'remote computing' is possible. In such a system, input facilities can be located at a long distance from the main processor of a computer system.

Communications in between the input and the output peripherals and the main computer can be maintained by a telephone or microwave transmission. In this system, several widely separated units located at different places can utilise the central computer facility. Usually, in such a system, appropriate programming is made, so that a computer can handle both local and remote demands.

The data entered at a remote online terminal are stored in the main computer memory and processed according to programmes designed for the particular purpose. In this case, all remote users get the service instantaneously at different locations at the same time, as and when required. When the central computer system pays attention to each remote terminal, all or several, in a specified time and operates simultaneously in a specified sequence instantaneously, it is called the 'time sharing' system. Each remote terminal gets the output in turn but considering the computer speed, a very small fraction of a second not perceptible by human sense, it is felt that the output is instantaneous.

In a time sharing system, each user has access to the computer when-ever he wants it. He can have access to a part of or the total storage of the main computer memory. He may even be assigned a storage area in the main computer and there he can keep his own programme for future use. In a time sharing system, a number of independent terminals located at various places is provided direct access to the central processor or the main computer. The system allows multiprogramming at a very high speed with one or more terminals. Special purpose time sharing computer systems are more and more being used in libraries both for library and information services so that a large number of users can use the system in various ways for different purposes.

Either the housekeeping jobs performed by the library staff or storage of data for information retrieval or current awareness service for the information scientist, or browsing over the library catalogue for information retrieval by users-any of or all such services can be rendered simultaneously by a time sharing computer system. Several terms are used to mean such a system. These are remote access, multi-processing, multi-programming, multi-access and the like.

The term 'multiprocessing computer system' is specifically used where the computer becomes an integral part of a complex operation rather than an instrument used for computation or processing. In the multiprocessing computer system, a single central processing unit having several input/output terminals is not used, but two or more central processing units are interconnected that serve all the input/output terminals of the system.

Online access may be available to local databases or external databases across geographical barriers. The searching is made through an online terminal connected, via the telecommunication network, to a host computer or a series of computers. Within a locality, a terminal can be hardware to the computer. For distant communications, a telecommunication network is required via either leased or dial-up lines.

When a database is needed through an international telecommunication network, access is made through a local node of network using a telephone. The local node is usually a minicomputer that transmits messages through a large computer network. Within a country, the ground communication is made via coaxial cables and microwave communication channels suitable for the computerised data network.

The satellite-earth stations are used for satellite telecommunication. The satellite control earth stations, equipped with the ground communication equipment, such as, the antennae, the tracking and telecommand equipment, communicate via the ground-satellite-ground communication via a satellite is the recent speediest channel of communication. There are many online system networks for access to many databases over the telecommunication network both for current information and retrospective databases.

Millions of document abstracts, serial titles, indexed data and information contained in thousands of documents may be available through a telephone call and a tele-typewriter, which is a device almost identical to an ordinary typewriter with additional keys for communicating with a computer. The electrical signals from the tele-typewriter are converted to audible signals that move through the telephone line and then the process is reversed for the messages on their way back.

These simple communication media have a profound impact on the communication technology, and tremendous progress has been made in respect of rapid access to any quantum of information. The earliest attempt for access to the computerised database was made in the mid-sixties by the US National Library of Medicine with the introduction of the batch processed database on medical science known as MEDLARS.

The provision to MEDLATS online is known as MEDLINE. The provision for access to online databases on a commercial basis was introduced by Lockheed under the name DIALOG and by the system

Development Corporation under the name ORBIT Online Retrieval of Bibliographic Information Time. Both Lockheed and SDC provide an enormous range of materials with a large number of data bases. Another commercial organisation is Bibliographic Retrieval Services started in 1976 in USA.

As for interlibrary lending, libraries relied on printed catalogs, telephones, mail and assorted other means of document delivery long before the vent of the computer. There is a logical continuum between these two services, both in their noncomputerized and their computer-assisted forms. Indexes and abstracts are likely to provide the library user with references to materials that are not available on the immediate premises, and it is at this point where an interlibrary loan service takes over.

In a constantly increasing number of libraries, subject-oriented printed indexes and abstracts, such as Chemical Abstracts, Sociological Abstracts, and Modern Language Association Bibliography, are being replaced or supplemented by online access to machine-readable versions of the same publication.

Use of these database is through a service agency that provides access to many such database. Simply by dialing a telephone number, a terminal in a library in connected via one of several telecommunications networks to the service agency's computer.

Through a simple identification, the searcher specifies which database on the computer is to be searched and then proceeds through interactive dialog to retrieve citations that are pertinent to a user's search request. Machine-readable database that are accessible in the manner described above and the computers on which they are stored are so numerous, so constantly changing, and so undocumented that they defy estimation. Discussion is limited here to services that have targeted libraries as a primary commercial concern. Even so, it is possible to arrive at meaningful estimates only by setting up fairly strict criteria for inclusion. Martha Williams, for example, estimate that by the end of the 1970s there were 650 "bibliographic-textual-natural language" data-bases searchable either online or in batch mode and "publicly available" on "major U.S. and Canadian bibliographic retrieval systems". These parameters make it somewhat easier to identify the major bibliographic retrieval systems and services within a library context.

In the past, very few actual producers of these databases-primarily the indexing and abstracting services-have felt it economically viable to offer online access themselves. Instead, thee producers have generally concentrated efforts on just creating machine-readable files of bibliographic information, the "raw material" for a retrieval system. The producer then license the machine-readable database to a database vendor which has developed a retrieval system and has mounted many such databases on its computers.

It is the vendor, then that provides libraries and other institutions online access to the content of the databases. Since most of the major vendors have this type of arrangement with a number of database producers, there are fewer database vendors than producers. In some, cases, the relationship between the information retrieval service the retrieval system it uses, and the database to which it offers accesses is fairly straight forward. For example. System Development Corporation (SDC) offers a service through its internally developed OR-BIT retrieval system, with access to more than 70 distinct database.

In other case, the relationship is less direct. For example, Bibliographic Retrieval Services (BRS), another major online service uses a version of the STAIRS system developed by IBM. Perhaps the most complex relationship, especially in a historical sense, concerns the National Library of Medicine (NLM), which acts both as a database producer and as a vendor of its own databases. The retrieval system used in NLM's own service is ELHILL-2; the earliest version was developed by SDC based in large part on ORBIT.

Adding to all this complexity is the fact that a number of the databases available from major vendors are not offered by only one service, but rather by two or three or more. For example, access to portions of NLM's most comprehensive database, MEDLARS, is offered not only by NLM directly but also through BRS and DIAIOG. The ERIC database complied by the National Institute of Education is offered through BRS, DIALOG, and SDC.

As one might expect in such cases of parallel service, there is a significant amount of professional literature that compares the retrieval effectiveness of professional literature that compares the retrieval effectiveness of different service for database offered through more than one service. Two of the practical advantages that online indexing and abstracting databases have over their printed counterparts are the same is in online technical processing systems and publications catalogue currency of information and flexibility in searching.

In terms of implementation, the earliest of the online technical processing systems, and even online public-access catalogs, predated use of formally established information retrieval services by libraries. This is not to say, however that the design of the latter was in any based on the former. The fact that the information retrieval services did not really emerge until the early 1970s in a publicly available forum was not clue to a lack of developed systems, but rather to other factors.

The various information retrieval services had several features in common that distinguished them from online library catalogues and systems for technical processing application. Some of these distinguishing features included:

1. Subject orientation, covering material pertinent to a particular discipline, in some cases narrowly defined and in others quite broadly defined, rather than the holdings of a particular library.
2. An emphasis on indexing and abstracting of the periodical literature rather than books.
3. An emphasis on remote access to centrally stored database by a number of different users.
4. Use limited to searching and retrieval of information; data in the master file could not be permanently added to or purged from the database by remote access users.

In addition, the vendor-based information retrieved systems of the 1970s and their predecessors in the 1960s shared a distinguishing emphasis in the direction of system capabilities. Almost without exception, the earliest online library operations systems of the 1960s were very rudimentary in certain features, such as depth of indexing of machine-stored records and breadth of retrieval capabilities for accessing those records.

In contrast, bibliographic storage and retrieval systems developed by the information retrieval services had placed their most concentrated focus on precisely those features so lacking in sophistication in the early online library systems. They are designed with primary emphasis on in-depth indexing of records and exploited the tremendous power of computers in order to provide more sophisticated avenues of retrieval.

One of the more successful initial efforts in the design of an online bibliographic retrieval system was in conjunction with the Technical Information Project (TIP) at the Massachusetts Institute of Technology in the early 1960s. The database created for the field of physics; by 1966, the database included about 35,000 citations. The input for each source article consisted of a citation that included the name of the journal, the issue and pagination on which it appeared, the author and title, the institutional affiliation of the author, and a list of all references cited in the article. The procedure for retrieving citations from the TIP database required the searcher first to specify the parameters of the search, such as which issues of which journal were to be searched.

Next, the user entered a search strategy, instructing the system to retrieve all citations of articles, for example by a given author or with appertain term in the title. Boolean searching could be performed and the system also allowed for retrieval on truncated search terms. In entering more than one term in a title search a user had the flexibility of specifying whether these terms had to appeal an anywhere within a title or whether they had to appear exactly in the same order as specified in the search statement. The decision not to assign additional subject descriptors for each article was based in part on the premise that if very sophisticated search and retrieval capabilities were designed into the system, subject-access avenues might be available that would not depend on manual selection and assignment of subject terms.

Such an experiment had profound implications for creating information retrieval database, for it reduced the input procedure to a clerical task not requiring the additional, purely intellectual, time and effort involved in selecting and assigning subject terms. The nontraditional form of subject access in the TIP system was based on manipulation of citations listed as references in source documents. A searcher could enter an author's name on title of a work and retrieve records for all source documents that had cited that author or titles as a reference. One extension of this capability was bibliographic coupling. A searching could enter two authors names or two titles. For example, and would retrieve records for all source documents that had cited both authors or both titles.

The premise for citation retrieval and bibliographic coupling as a form of subject access was that there exists a strong correlation between the subject article and the subject of works cited therein. Further, the more references any two articles have in common, the before closely related the subject of those two articles are likely to be. For a searcher who was aware of important works in a particular field that were likely to be cited, these retrieval capabilities represented a viable form of subject access.

Recognizing that this was only a partial approach and would have assumed that the user was already aware off articles likely to be cited, the TIP retrieval system design incorporated features that automatically assisted the search process. A most interesting strategy was a set of procedures referred to in TIP as Strategy A. The user did not have to execute all of the steps involved, but merely had to initiate the strategy by entering a search term that was likely to appear in titles of source documents on a subject in which he or she was interested. After retrieving records for all source documents with this term in the title, the system automatically examined all references cited in those documents and ranked the references according the number of documents citing them. Given a cut-off point the system then took the most commonly cited references and searched for other source documents in the database, which even though lacking the original search term in their title, cited these same references.

Once this second file of source documents was complied and added to the first, the system then examined all titles to identify the most frequently appearing terms apart from the original search term. It then went back through the entire database to retrieve still other source documents with these secondary terms in their titles. This interplay continued until no new records were retrieved. In addition to citation-retrieval and bibliographic-coupling techniques such as those designed into the TIP system, other retrieval techniques developed during the 1960s explored the computer's potential for elimination the need for human indexing and at the same time for assisting in making judgment about the relevance of records in the database to any given search query. In contrast, a number of other experimental systems were designed in which human indexing of source documents played an integral role.

The retrieval effectiveness of these systems was evaluated with regard to such variables as depth of indexing, selection of index terms form various portions of the source documents, use of controlled versus uncontrolled indexing vocabulary, and construction of thesauri.

The 1960s were indeed an exciting period for exploring a broad range of issues related to bibliographic storage and retrieval on computers. A more detailed discussion of these issue and the specific retrieval techniques and systems developed to study them during the 1960s is beyond the scope of this book, but a source that may be of interest, and particularly appropriate for developments during that decade, is Lancaster's and Fayen's Information Retrieval On-Line.

The sophisticated techniques devised for the TIP project and for other system during the 1960s provided the theoretical basis that would be used in the early 1970s. Some of the vendors of that time had, in act, been in the forefront of information retrieval systems design during the 1960s. Of the systems developed in those years, the two that have had the most long-standing impact on libraries are the DIALOG system, developed by the Lockheed Corporation, and the ORBIT system, by System Development Corporation (SDC). By 1964, the Information Science Group at Lockheed's Palo Alto, California, Research Laboratory was experimenting with an online information retrieval system called CONVERSE. In its initial version, CONVERSE was a primitive effort compared with what it would soon lead to. Searching a database of 100 document citations, experimenters selected prepunched cards on which possible search terms had been recorded, and read these "search cards" into the system through a one-card reader. The system searched the database to find records on a teletype machine, showing either full bibliographic information for each citation retrieved or only the document citation reference number, depending on the number of citations retrieved. If the search retrieved more than 15 citations, the system sent a message to this effect and the searcher had to refine the search strategy.

By 1967, through constant refinement and introduction of more so-phisticated capabilities, CONVERSE was transformed into DIALOG, The impetus for the initial application of DIALOG was Lockheed's contract with the National Aeronautic and Space Administration (NASA) to develop a remote retrieval capability for the NASA data-base, to be used by the NASA Ames Research Center in California. A year earlier, NASA had awarded a contract to the Bunker-Ramo Corporation for development of a prototype system to allow three other NASA centers remote access to a NASA database stored in Bunker-Ramo's computer in New York City. The 300,000 citation NASA database was mounted on a computer a Lockheed's Palo Alto facility.

A remote-access terminal was placed at the Ames Research Center, from which engineers and scientists accessed the database through the DIALOG retrieval language. A subsequent contract was awarded to Lockheed to provided similar retrieval system that could be mounted at NASA's own facilities. The resulting system, called RECON (Remote Console), was base largely on DIALOG. The rights for future development of RECON were retained by NASA, and in the early 1970s, NASA in fact removed its database storage from, NASA awarded the contract for maintenance and further development of the RECON system to Informatics, Inc., a Lock-heed competitor during the early 1970s in the emerging information retrieval services industry. The System Development Corporation had participated in the design of interactive retrieval systems as early as 1960. This experimental retrieval system, called PROTOSYNTHEX, incorporated full-text searching capability with the text of Golden Book Encyclopedia serving as its database. During the mid-1960s. SDC continued to work on the design of online information retrieval systems. One result was BOLD (Bibliographic On-Line Display) which was tested on a database several thousand bibliographic records and abstracts for technical reports issued by the United State

Documentation Center. Another SDC system during that period was COLEX (Central Information Reference and Control On-Line Experimentation), used by the Foreign Technology Division of the U.S. Air Force Systems Command at Wright-Patterson Air Force Base in Ohio.

ORBIT (On-Line Retrieval of Bibliographic Information Time-shared) emerged at SDC from experiences gained through the design of such system as BOLD and COLEX. An important development in SDC's information retrieval systems history occurred in 1970 when it was awarded a contract by the National Library of Medicine (NLM). The contract called for a portion of NLM's MEDLARS machine-readable database to be loaded on a computer a SDC's facilities in Santa Monica, California, and for SDC to develop a retrieval system and to provide remote access to approximately 30 libraries and hospitals throughout the United States. The project came to be known as AIM-TWX (Abridged Index Medicus Teletype Writer Exchange Network). Much as Lockheed had done for NASA, SDC developed a retrieval system specifically for use with the MEDLARS database. Given the name ELHILL the system was very similar to SDC's own ORBIT.

Beginning in June 1970, the AIM-TWX service enabled any of the participating institutions to dial into SDC's computer over the TWX or standard telephone network and conduct online searches of the NLM database using the ELHILL retrieval language. In 1971, after months of experience with the AIM-TWX project, NLM mounted a portion of the MEDLARS database on its own computer and, using the ELHILL system, established its own online search service called MEDLARS file mounted on its computers and accessible through ORBIT.

In the mid-1870s, however, NLM terminated that arrangement and withdrew its database from SDC. Among information retrieval systems development during the 1960s, ORBIT and DIALOG eventually had the greatest impact on the broadest range of libraries. Another important system appeared late in the decade that would gain library use-the Mead Data Central system developed by Mead Corporation. Its first applications were in providing online access to the Ohio Bar Automated Research (OBAR) legal database of the Ohio State Association, the Epilepsy Abstracts Retrieval System (EARS) database provided by the National Institute of Neurological Diseases and Stroke, and the machine-readable bibliographic files of the National Technical Information Service.

Mead narrowed its scope during the 1970s, concentrating largely on providing access to LEXIS, an outgrowth of OBAR, and to NEXIS, a news-oriented database. Application of online retrieval systems during the 1960s were generally limited to use in government agencies and by corporations. Probably the first Information retrieval "service" used by libraries other than in those agencies or corporations was not provided by Lockheed or SDC, but the State University of New York Biomedical Communications Network (SUNY BCN). Under the direction of Irwin Pizer SUNY BCN became access via direct telephone lines to a database storied on a computer at the SUNY Upstate Medical Center in New York.

The libraries included seven in New York State, the Country Library of Medicine at Harvard, and the National Library of Medicine. As information retrieval services emerged in the early 1970s, SUNY BCN was somewhat distinctive in that it was neither the major producer of the database used nor the developer of the information retrieval system used to access it. The original retrieval system used was the Document

Processing System (DPS) developed by IBM, replaced in 1973 by IBM's STAIRS (Storage and Information Retrieval System). Although it is true that the database was in part created by direct input from member libraries, much of it consisted of MEDLARS records provided by the National Library of Medicine. The SUNY BCN database was broader in purpose than those eventually accessible through other information retrieval services. By 1969, it included MEDLARS files dating back to 1964, bibliographic records for monographs and serials titles cataloged by NLM since 1967, for all monographs cataloged in three of the participating libraries since 1962, for a portion of monographs cataloged by the Countway Library since 1968, and records for a 25,000-title union list of serials held libraries on campuses of State University of New York and in several others.

Not all of this data was permanently available online, but requests for searching the file stored offline could be submitted over the same terminal used for online searching. These requests were then batch searched and the results mailed. In terms of retrieval capabilities the early version of the IBM Documented Processing System was not as sophisticated as some of the systems being developed elsewhere. Once entered, a search could not be interrupted by the user until it was completely processed.

Even more restrictive the system could return only ten citations in response to any search query. If the search retrieved more than ten citations, the system printed out only the ten most recently published. If the user wished to see more than ten, the search strategy could be reentered and processed again to retrieve ten more citations. This was on awkward and time-consuming procedure, particularly since the terminals communicated at comparatively slow speeds.

Many of the design limitations imposed by the IBM Document Processing System were alleviated when SUNY BCN converted to the STAIRS System. SUNY BCN grew from its original 9 participants in 1968 to 32 by 1973 and continued in operation until 1977. As is evident from the description of the early information retrieval systems and services that were to have the strongest impact on libraries, the machine-readable MEDLARS database played a key role in their development.

By late 1971, the MEDLARS database or portions of it were available though at least three different services: SDC, SUNY BCN, and the National Library of Medicine itself. NLM may have had one of the largest bibliographic machine-readable databases, but other government agencies were also creating such files and mounting them for information retrieval were also creating such files and mounting them cress with the NASA project, was in the forefront of providing government agencies with retrieval services through the DIALOG system. In 1969, it mounted the Nuclear Science Abstract database for use by the Atomic Energy Commission and the ERIC database containing machine-readable records for citations in Research in Education and Current Index to Journals in Education for use by the U.S. Department of Education.

Between 1970 and 1972, other information retrieval services began providing access to database created by government agencies: SDC made the ERIC database available through ORBIT; Mead briefly provided access to the NTIS database; and Informatics, Inc, maintain the TOXICON (later TOXLINE) retrieval system for National Library of Medicine. Of equal important to the increase in the number of database produced by government agencies was the mounting of nongovernment databases by the information retrieval services.

By 1972, SDC was offering online access through ORBIT to the Chemical Abstracts Condensates database; Mead was offering access to the Psychological Abstracts database; and Lockheed was providing access to PANDEX created by the McMillan Company and covering scientific and technical literature. During the early 1970s, online access to at least some of these data bases was becoming publicly available. In essence, any institution could gain access if it was willing to pay the fees charged by the service on whose computers the database stored. But there were a couple of problems that stood in the way of an immediately outburst of enthusiasm on the part of librarians. One was a basic unfamiliarity with such services, their technology and the procedures involved. Beyond this however, was the question of costs, and most particularly of communications costs.

In accessing a database through one of these service, it was necessary to dial the computer via standard telephone lines or in some cases, through a TWX network. Since the service's central computer might be located at some distance, this was not an inexpensive venture, and communications costs could comprise a substantial portion of the total cost of the search. This obstacle was partially overcome during the early 1970s with the introduction of public accessible packet-switching networks, such as TYMNET and TELENET. Circuit-switched networks, such as used for telephone and TWX communication, reserved a fixed bandwidth over which communication occurs for the entire duration of a connection.

Packet switching, on the other hand, sends messages over communications networks in smaller blocks of information. It ideally suite for communication in a computer network, since the network is activated for any particular user only when a message is ready to be sent. It does not maintain a permanent connection between points over a field bandwidth during the entire course of a communication, which would include time spent in formulating search strategy, keying the strategy, computer processing of a request, and so on. Extensive research on the cost-effectiveness of packet-switching communications networks had been conducted by Rand as early as 1964 Commissioned by the U.S.

Air Force to conduct a feasibility study the Rand Corporation in fact recommended that the Air Force adopt such a network, which would not only be less expensive but would also provide a defensively more secure communication network than was available through existing systems. The Air Force adopt also provide a defensively more secure communication network than was available through existing systems. The Air force did not act on the recommendation. In the Late 1960s, however, the Advanced Research Projects Agency (ARPA) of the U.S. Department of Defense funded development of a packet-switching network. By December 1969, ARPANET was declared operational, linking four computers located at deferent sites.

In the late 1960s and early 1970s work proceeded on establishing similar network for a broader audience of users. These efforts culminate in the formation of the TYMNET and TELENET network the latter created by some of the people who had worked on ARPANET. Each of these "value added" networks established nodes in a number of major U.S. cities. Each node consisted of a minicomputer, which acted as a communications link and as an interface device between remote terminals and host computers, such as those on which database were being stored at Lockheed and SDC.

In order establish a connection between a terminal and a host computer the user still had to dial into the computer but in using TYMNET and TELENET, the standard telephone link occurred only between the terminal and the minicomputer at the nearest network node. Messages received by the minicomputer were then sent over telephone lines leased by the networks to another node, and so on through the network until the message reaches the host computer. Messages returned from a host computer to a remote terminal followed the same procedure. The exact route any message might take through the networks was determined dynamically by the network itself and depended on the flow of traffic at the precise moment of communication. The bottom line of the packet-switching networks was that they dramatically reduced telecommunication costs. As a measure of the magnitude by which these costs were reduced, Devis McCarn at the National Library of Medicine estimated in 1974 that with the introduction of packet-switching networks, the average cost of communications for MEDLINE searching immediately dropped from $24 per hour to $5 per hour- a decrease of about 80 percent. A further innovation was the pricing structure.

Unlike the telephone system, the packet-switching networks charged a flat hourly rate for communications, regardless of which node a message emanated from and regardless of where it was sent. During the same period that the packet-switching networks were being introduced commercially, computer hardware costs were declining sharply. This was no small consideration for the information retrieval service as they added new database to their collections. By mid-1974 for example, SDC was offering service on about 11 database with a collective 3.5 million bibliographic records. These require in the vicinity of 3.3 billion bytes of storage on disks that had a capacity of 200 million bytes each 11. These dual-density disk were in fact a relatively recent breakthrough on the market, improving upon disks that had a storage capacity in the range of only half that amount. The decrease in costs for telecommunications and per-unit computer storage brought the price of these service into a more acceptable range for libraries and other institutions. As the number of users began to grow and maintenance and development cost could be distributed across a large number of users, prices decreased still further.

The increased revenues, in turn, could be used to license new databases and make additional enhancements in order to attract still more users. As an indication of the total impact of these and other factors on pricing during the early 1970s, the cost of searching through Lockheed's service in 1973 was less than half of what it had been in 1970, and between and 1973 and 1975 the cost was again reduced by about half. Although it is difficult to trace the magnitude by which the use of information retrieval services grew during the 1970s, one is to examine the growth of the service themselves.

In 1971 there were less than half a dozen services that offered access to bibliographic databases, and each of those had only between one and three database available. Lockheed and SDC each offered service to more than ten databases, and NLM had broadened the number as well, although some were essentially spin-offs from the main MEDLARS file. SUNY BCN continued its service and in fact entered an arrangement with NLM for its computer to act as a backup for searching MEDLARS. One of the new services to appear in the early 1970 was the New York Times Information Bank (NYTIB). Its database had been available for in-house use at the New York

Time office since 1971. In 1973 access became publicly available exclusively through the Times own new commercial information retrieval service, using a retrieve language designed by IBM.

Coverage included not only articles from the New York Times dating back to the late 1960s, but also selects items from more than 60 other newspapers and periodicals indexed back to 1971. The depth of the NYTIB indexing was extremely through, based on the use of a controlled vocabulary. The was at time cause for annoyance, especially given the fact that this database was a source of material on current events. One user, for example wrote of the frustration in attempting to retrieve articles about migration to the "sunbelt states" at a time of extensive news coverage of that phenomenon. The controlled vocabulary used by the NYTIB did not include such a term, nor did it have any term that corresponded to the geographic area being described. Although the descriptor "Southern Rim State (LS)" was eventually added to the list of acceptable index terms and an attempt made to reindex some of the material in the database retrospectively with this term, such efforts required time. This aspect off a controlled vocabulary was certainly not unique to the NYTIB; it is one faced by any database using a controlled vocabulary for searching. Martha Williams estimated that in 1974 approximately 700,000 online searches were conducted in the United States on remote-access bibliographic retrieval systems other than OCLC.

To illustrate how pivotal a period this was for the commercial information retrieval service, in December 1972, SDC could claim less than one-half dozen organizations using its searching service. Within six months, this number had grown to more than 40, and by early 1974 the number of subscribers approaches 150. Another author stated that the number of searches on Lockheed's DIALOG in 1975 was more than seven times the number conducted in 1973. Already by 1974, there sere more than 500 organizations searching MEDLARS through either NLM or SUNY BCN services, and Cuadra estimates that in 1975, 18 well over 2,000" organisations were conducting searches through the various on line information retrieval services. With such a rapid growth rate, there were constant changes and new problem. One very basic problem for the service themselves has how, despite advances in technology, to keep their computer configurations of sufficient size to handle the enormous number of machine-readable records included in the databases to which they offered access.

One solution was to maintain records online only for the most recently published materials, often a two- to five-year span. SDC used an approach whereby database were rotated during the course of each day, making some available for the entire day but others for only a few hours, a decision that resulted in a one-half to two-thirds savings in storage costs over what would have been necessary had all databases been mounted all the time the system was available. Between the mid-and late 1970s, the information retrieval services continued to grow. The years 1975 through 1977 saw some fundamental changes and controversies in the information retrieval service industry.

By 1975, the National Library of Medicine, although continuing to provide SUNY BC with its MEDLARS file, had withdrawn MEDLARS from SDC and TOXLINE from Informations, Inc, SDC, of course, already had a broad range of other databases. Informatics, meanwhile, attempted to expand its services by offering online access to the Excerpta Medica database compiled by the Excerpta Medica

Foundation in Amsterdam. There was significant continued to offer Excerpta Media for several years, it was an uphill battle all the way. NLM and its MEDLARS database were subsidized operation, and Roger Summit of Lockheed tersely observed the resulting impact on competition in 1975: "NLM with MEDLARS and Informatics with Excerpta Medica are in competition at prices of $15 ($8 of shift) and $120 per hour respectively. NLM was not the only government agency whose direction was of concern to the commercial services during the mid-1970s.

In 1975, for example the U.S. Energy and Research Development Association (ERDA) began offering a restricted group of government agencies several databases that were also being offered through commercial services, but FRDA's charges were far lower. The commercial services saw government subsidization as the reason for the wide discrepancies in pricing between their services and those offered through the public agencies for searching the same databases. In 1976, a significant new commercial enterprise announced plans to enter the information retrieval business. In its Final Prospectus, the Bibliographic Retrieval Service (BRS) explained its rationale as follows:

At the end of 1975, a survey of the available online database search services disclosed that the existence of a wide gap between the cost of those services available from the public sector (government and university services) and those for sale by private information companies.

Access to the public services was generally at cost-recovery levels, averaging between $10 and $15 per connect hour, including communications costs, while the cost of accessing commercial services ranged from $25 to $150 per connect hour, excluding communications costs.

Unfortunately the online services provided by the public sector were limited either by their narrow subject scope or regional communication networking, and yet the comparatively high cost of commercial services precluded many interested libraries from using them as an alternative supplier. Thus the information needs of a major segment of the potential user base for these new services were simply not being met.

The BRS was established to fill this gap by making it possible for the national community of libraries online at connect hour ranging from as low as $10 per hour to a maximum of $30 per hour. The idea behind the formation of BRS, and indeed even some of its staffing, stemmed from SUNY BCN which phased out its services a few months after BRS began operations in early 1977.

Using the IBM STAIRS retrieval system, BRS provided an initial offering of ten databases. Two were MEDLARS and TOXLINE from NLM; the remaining eight covered a rather broad range of topics, and each was also available through either DIALOG, SDC, or both. Another new service on the market in 1977 was Dow Jones News/Retrieval (DJNR). Its database consisted of items appearing on the Dow Jones News Wire, in the Wall Street Journal, and in Barron's magazine. The appearance of DJNR was part of a significant trend beginning in the 1970s and continuing into the 1980s, which saw a number of news, financial, and popular literature databases enter the market with few notable exceptions, databases of this type had been conspicuously absent up to this time.

Most of these newly emerging producers chose not to go the route of DJNR setting up their own services, but rather vended their databases to one of the existing major services. One of the most successful new producers to emerge in the late 1970s was Information Access Corporation (IAC), first with its Magazine Index (MI) database and soon after with its National Newspaper Index (NNI). Both became available on DIALOG.

The MI indexed nearly 400 popular periodicals, including not coincidentally, all those covered in the Reader's Guide to Periodical Literature, published by the H.W. Wilson Company. NNI coverage included the Wall Street Journal, the Christian Science Monitor and, quite interestingly, the New York Times. Beginning in the Mid-1970s, Martha Williams monitored the growth of library-related information retrieval services and databases through the maintenance of a Database of Databases. The growth of the Data base of Databases during the second half of the industry.

Whereas 177 U.S. databases were recorded in the Database of Databases in 1975, the number had grown to 208 by 1977 and 259 by 1979. An even greater rate of growth occurred in the number of non U.S. databases, from 124 in 1975, to 154 in 1977 and to 269. The number off records available on these databases also showed impressive growth, from about 46 million in 1975 to 93.5 million by 1979 on non U.S. databases.

One must remember, too that these figures were only for bibliographic databases available through major online retrieval services and subject to other criteria for inclusion as well. Not all the database or records included in William's statistics were available for online searching; some were accessible only offline. It is indicative of the intensity of activity during that period that while in 1977 only about 47 percent of the records on both U.S. and non-U.S. databases were available online, this proportion had increased to 83 percent by 1979. The number of online searches of databases through major U.S. and Canadian systems, according to Williams, just about doubled ever two years during the last half of the 1970s.

In 1975, about I million online searches were conducted through these services; in 1977, there were approximately 2 million, and in 1979, about 4 million. During the 1980s, the information retrieval service industry has continued to grow. Several new services have emerged, and scores of new databases have appeared that are of central interest to libraries. Their use of these services and database has also continued to increase. But the changes in the information retrieval service industry have not simply been a matter of expansion in numbers. There has been innovation in form and content as well as increased competition, and recent and merging technologies have presented a host of new challenges and opportunities.

The first half of the 1980s has seen the microcomputer become almost commonplace in libraries, and these machines are being used in new and interesting ways in connection with online searching. By 1984, the ability to sore enormous amounts of text on compact devices-optical disks, in particular-is no longer a vision of the future but a reality of the present.

Online full text data-bases-containing not just citations to documents, but the entire text of the documents themselves- number more than just a few and the quantity is increasing.

Several other online library systems in the USA are OCLC at Ohio, BALLOTS at Stanford university, WLN at Olympia, RLIN. In Canada, the largest online computerised library system is UTLAS. In Britain, the largest online system is BLAISE. BLAISE offers online services through a large number of databases under various names and styles, such as MEDLINE, SDILINE, TOXLINE, CHEMLINE, CANCERLINE. In Europe, online access is available to ESA and DIMDI. The North American telecommunication networks are TYMNET and TELENET. They have more than 200 nodes in Europe and other parts of the world. The nearest point to India is at Hong Kong.

These networks provide access to almost all the major American online services. EURONET provides online service to EEC countries mainly, but it is begin extended to other countries also buy interconnecting with the host computer systems for such countries.

In India, online interconnection with ESA has been made on an experimental basis. Online searching is performed through an online terminal. The user must have a clear idea of the request, a chosen database and the online system with operational capability. The search comprises a series of keywords together with the Boolean or weighted-term logic. The search strategy of the search statement should be framed before logging-on.

When the communication is made by logging-on, the data of system will be displayed on the screen of the terminal and the user will be requested to select the required database. As the search proceeds, the interaction between the machine and the user goes on, and the user gives a series of commands to which the computer responds. The terminal is the visual display unit which has a cathode-ray tube (CRT) display.

A modern terminal is fitted with a continuous printer because it is necessary to get continuous printed record of searches. The printer is capable of working in parallel with VDU. The terminal is connected with the computer. But in between the terminal and the computer, a telephone connection is essential via a modem. Modem means 'Modulator Demodulator'. The function of a modem is to convert the digital messages, which both the terminal and the computer understand, to messages which are understandable trough the telephone. A similar device is connected with the computer at its end of communication. The computer must be connected with the telephone line like the standard telephone set. The telephone line should be a direct outside line, so that the connection is not interrupted by ordinary telephone calls and other noises in the line. While in operation, the printer prints the hard copy of the search. If the connection is for long distance international search, the telecommunication networks make the connection with the help of the nearest connection node. When the public telephone lines are used for connecting the computer, it is known as dial-up access.

Online selective dissemination of information service has been possible owing to random access searching and random access memory to keep users' profiles. The current information is made input under specific areas as required, and the prepared existing files are updated at regular intervals as and when needed to prepare the data files for SDI.

In libraries and information centers where SDI services are offered, an adequate number of profiles is maintained and online profiles are developed by the input and editing systems. SDI service sets are a series of unique data sets of references of infoımation with each set matching with one profile. These unique data sets may consist of reference numbers only or full bibliographic citations or full bibliographic citations with supplemented abstracts. These may be from various sources, but are arranged logically.

If a user has a terminal, he can get the SDI service directly online. If he does not have a terminal, the online SDI service output may be supplied to him by online printouts. The SDI service is a personalised information service. It is a sophisticated form of current awareness service on a selective area basis, so that the user can get up-to-date information for a specific purpose. The service requires a tremendous speed for collection, storage and retrieval of information, and an online system is best suited to get the desired result.

Computerises SDI service was initiated by H.P. Luhn in the early 1960s, while he was working in the IBM corporation. The titles of the documents used in the chemical abstracts were provide on magnetic tapes in 1962. The institute for scientific information first started SDI service on a commercial basis known as Automatic subject citation alert.

Since then, the computerised online SDI service has been being widely used. Some of the SDI services are: Canadian SDI operated by the Canadian institute for scientific and technical information and used in India; computer assisted information retrieval system used at the Leatherhead food research association; storage and information centre; Agricultural system for the storage and subsequent selection of information used at ICI.

In the mid-sixties, the National Library of Medicine in the USA produced the printed Index Medicus. The data were kept in the computer-readable form and the files were known as Medlars. These databases were generated files of computer-readable bibliographic description in the batch process for access to offline searching. The database of Medlars is available on online search service and the service is known as Medline which was wet up in 1973. The software is known as Elhill.

The national library of medicine offers online bibliographic search service now with more sophisticated software. It has also several online search services on medical information in several specific areas besides medicine in general. Sdiline contains the latest month's references to be used primarily for current awareness. Toxline consists of ten separate collections of secondary information in the fields of toxicology and environmental pollution.

CHEMLINE is an online dictionary file which enables the users of TOXLINE to describe chemical substances before beginning a search. The mesh vocabulary file contains information on all terms in the mesh thesaurus and it can be searched online.

The online system with the search language DIALOG is a commercially accessible online database operated by Lockheed information services at Palo alto in California, USA. It uses an IBM 360/65 computer with the software DIALOG. The software was prepared from the Recon soft-ware developed by lockheed for the national aeronautics and space agency, USA.

The online services of dialog comprise more than seventy databases on a wide range of human knowledge from agriculture, engineering, technology to humanities, social sciences, the arts, public affairs, management, economics and information science. It has databases, both bibliographic and non-bibliographic, American and European. It charges access fee, telecommunication charges and prices for printouts of retrieved references. Some of the databases are AGRICOLA, LISA, METADEX, SCISEARCH, SOCIAL SCISEARCH, CA condensates, COMPENDEX, ERIC, etc. DIALOG is an outstanding, successful online system and a principal leader in the online service.

With wide publicity in Europe it created a tremendous impact on computerised library and information services in Europe, and it has made significant contribution to online service in Europe. It has consultation facilities and it offers a wide range of boolean search options according to the requirements of users. DIALOG contains over 16 million bibliographic citations available online, and these are constantly being reviewed and updated.

A dialog search is expressed through search words or thesaurus terms with the commands like EXAPAND, SELECT, COMNINE and TYPE. The command or instruction is made input through an online terminal keyboard for processing by the computer. The output is displayed on the screen and then the searcher can proceed can proceed with the next command or can modify his search by the interactive method.

The system development corporation is also a pioneer like lockheed for commercially accessible online services. It is located at Santa Monica, California, USA. SDC and lockheed are the two largest online database organisations in the world. Both of them prepare purpose-built software and render online services through international telecommunication networks to many countries. SDC prepared a software package for online searching in 1968 known as orbit. It has over fifty databases. It uses and IBM 370/158 computer.

Orbit facilities and capabilities are constantly being reviewed and improved for purpose-oriented user needs. Some of the databases available through ORBIT are ACCOUNTANTS, AGRICOLA, BIOSIS, CAS 77, CHEMDEX, ENERGYLINE, ENVIROLINE, ERIC, INSPEC, NTIS, TITUS, etc. For user orientation ORBIT user manual and orbit quick reference guide are most useful. ORBIT has over 12 million bibliographic citations online.

The European Space Agency (ESA) operates network links with many computer installations in various European countries. Its UK node is located at the technology reports centre of the department of industry in Kent. It offers access to the space documentation service of esa. ESA formerly used the software package known as RECON, and the online database was known as ESA/RECON. The information retrieval service of the European space agency used ESA/RECON. At present, the version of recon has been revised and the software package is now known as QUEST.

The ESA/IRS database system provides access via online process to more than twenty databases mainly on nuclear and space sciences. IRS uses and IBM 360/65 computer located at Frascati near Rome. IRD can be used through the linking of leased line network by member countries. The department of Industry, U.K., provided a dial-up technical information service known as DIALTECH introduced by the Technology report centre in 1976. This service extended facilities to any user in the UK to dial the node at TRC and be connected to the ESA network having head-quarters in Frascati. The node at trc in kent is a minicomputer and the search method is QUEST.

The information retrieval service at Frascati can be accessed online from various locations via telecommunication networks like TIMESHARE ESANET and others. The database includes INSDEC, CONPENDEX, NASA, POLLUTION and the like. The simple access through the ordinary telephone lines to large databases in computer-readable from has been possible, and can be used online. The operational information retrieval service network of the European space agency is the largest European network. It is now known as ESAANET. It serves usually the west European countries.

ESANET is planning to provide ready and equal access to scientific and technical information for all member countries of the European economic community through international telecommunication networks. Thus, online data service and information exchange can be possible among all the member countries.

EURONET is a European online information service operating to offer access to a large number of databases and the sharing of resources among the member countries of the European economic community. It envisages generation of databases in the member countries, as well as access to online databases across geographical boundaries of the member countries. The countries are interconnected by the online system for sharing of information and online information retrieval.

A system has been devised known as DIANE which offers online search service using the packet-switching data transmission network, with such latest technology, information is transmitted in 'packets' by switching operation. It is fast, reliable and effective on available lines, and it makes automatic corrections of transmission errors. A large number of databases created in the member countries and other online agencies, such as MEDLINE, DIALOG, ORBIT, CANCERLINE, INIS, ISDS, NASA, etc., is available in EURONET. A common command language has been devised that will help the existing sophisticated language as an alternative. The system of packet switching ensures more efficient use of available lines, a large range of terminals compatible with the network and the most effective and efficient service transmission errors are corrected automatically and the network provides alternative routes. It is also inexpensive.

EURONET is interconnected by a large number of European host computers and makes them accessible from any part of the continent. Many host online computer networks are interconnected in EURONET, such as BLAISE, INFOLINE, ESA IRS, information retrieval service, DIMDI, and online host systems of other member countries.

TELENET is an online network operated by bolt, Baranek and Newman in north America. Lockheed and the system development corporation databases can be accessed via this network in the European countries through trans-Atlantic tele-communications.

TYMNET is a network operated by timeshare inc. The network having online services is based in north America, but it has telecommunication access to several nodes in Europe. Lockheed and sdc databases can be accessed also by this online network to European countries. Both the online networks, telenet and tymnet, were implemented in the early seventies in north America and were accessible to Europe and other counties of the world.

They have more than 200 nodes in north America and several nodes in Europe in London, Paris, Rome, Viennna, Geneva, the hague, breussels, Frankfurt and other cities, as well as in other cities in Asia and south America like hong kong, manila, Singapore, San Juan etc. When a number of libraries, as a group of participating institutions, work for organised collection of resources and for rendering planned, coordinated services to a wider section of users interconnected by communication channels it is said to form a library network.

The network is formed to achieve better sharing of resources, both acquisition and collection of library materials, as well as bibliographic data recordings. Library automation, growth of computer technology and advances in communication technology have facilitated library networks to render better services.

In online information retrieval the searcher uses a computer terminal usually linked by telephone to a remote computer. The computer stores the database of bibliographic records on rotating magnetic disks always available for immediate access. The database can be searched and re-searched using special computer programs which allow the searcher to carry out a two-way conversation or dialogue with the computer.

Online retrieval offers many advantages, the following being particularly noteworthy:

— In-depth searches of computer-held files can be carried out at a speed which no human can hope to match.

— The user is an active participant and can instantly adapt his request to the reality of what is actually in the reference file-perhaps very different from what he expects-and also readily recover from errors in the formulation of queries.

— Databases can easily be re-searched, using new clues.

— The user has easy access to an extremely wide range of indexes and databases, many of which may not be available locally.

— Databases searchable online often offer a far greater number of access points than the corresponding printed indexes.

— There is almost no need for the irksome note-taking so typical of many conventional searches.

There is continuing growth in availability of SDI services from most online suppliers. Generally, the user's interest profile is held in an online file and matched against the incoming information. The resulting list of current references matching the user's profile can as an admirable way to keep up-to-date. Developments in the supply of SDI services are taking place so rapidly that this Directory makes no attempt to provide details since they would be misleading by the time this text reaches the reader. Up-to-date details can easily be obtained from the main suppliers. However, some idea of the wide range of databases from which SDI service can be drawn can be seen which shows a selection of DIALOG files with automatic SDI capability.

It should be noted that the word "database" is often used outside the library and information field to describe any set of computer-held structured records which can be approached using search keys, and that the word "databank" is sometimes used synonymously. In the field of library and information science the words database and databank are now usually taken to have the following meanings: a database generally provides details of bibliographic references which the searcher uses as keys in order to consult the original source literature to obtain the detailed knowledge he is seeking.

Increasingly, the online record will contain an abstract, or indeed full-text detail, which answers the enquirer's question without reference to other documentation; a databank, on the other hand, concentrates on factual information and generally gives a direct answer without further reference to original source documents. For example, a statistical tabulation of the output from British coal mines over the last century can easily be loaded into an online file; at a later time a question concerning the output in a specific year produces a specific numerical quantity which the enquirer can immediately use as a "fact".

Online databases are usually a by-product arising from the computer-production of conventional printed indexes. Typically, the databases producer/owner makes available magnetic tapes for lease or for sale, usually in a format based on, or deriving from, the producer's, in-house requirements for the production of the printed abstracting journal. Generally, these tapes contain a set of complete bibliographic records, each record being described by the contents of a number of data "fields. The fields used, and the order in which they appear, will vary from producer to producer but may contain some or all of the following:

A = Inter-record gap

B = Start-of-record marker

C = In-house header handling details

D = Database producer's accession number

E = Name of author

F = Corporate author

G = Title

H = Abstract

I = Section heading

J = Controlled thesaurus terms

K = Uncontrolled free-indexing terms

l = Notes

M = Additional in-house handling details

N = Extra field for the specific database

O = End-of-record marker

P = Inter-record gap

The above listing is for the purposes of illustration only; it is not intended as the profile for an average database. The magnetic tapes supplied by database producers are often leased/sold at prices which in terms of a unit-record are very cheap indeed. For example, the METADEX tapes are available at $5-$20 per record. But of course the in-house record can be expected to be nearly 100% germane to the interests of the creating body; bought-in tapes will clearly contain much redundant material. "Downloading" from a service supplier's online database, having selected wanted references, clearly has many cost and effort advantages in cases where it is legal to download.

Overall, the immense size of producers' production costs is little appreciated by users; VINKEN estimated the global costs of abstracting and indexing publications for eventual storage on databases at $80 million per year. An online service supplier on receiving such tapes will generally use an in-house reformatting computer program to read the tape and reformat the data-elements as received into a new format appropriate to the online inverted file and retrieval programs used by that specific online service. The reformatted records are then loaded into the online service supplier's retrieval system. A "standard" record sent out on a magnetic tape will thus be handled differently on different online service suppliers' systems.

4

CD-ROM Networks

The CD-ROM has been the high flier of the late 1980s and will continue to change the way that we operate as librarians well into the 90s. In 1987 two libraries indicated that they were considering using CD-ROM while in 1989, 49 were actually in the thick of it. A variety of databases were being used, but all were using Bookbank which was the catalyst for most libraries. In four years the number has gone up 50 times, since 1989 it has more than doubled.

CD-ROM is a popular delivery system for information and is likely to continue its sweep through public libraries. The data are pretty self-evident, there are increases everywhere. A wide range of databases are now in use, ranging from those of local relevance, such as the Northern Echo, to national newspapers, official publications, British Standards and the odd encyclopedia.

Selection tools remain a popular sue for the CD-ROM equipment and alongside Bookbank we now find Bookfind, American Books in Print, BNB and the British Library Catalogue. Respondents were asked to indicate whether the systems were staff only or made available directly to the public, without staff intervention. Of the 101 total, 66 indicated that their systems were staff only while nine report direct use by the public. That leaves 26 who said nothing about access. From the databases the 26 'question marks' are using, they are not providing public access, which means that only about one tenth of CD-ROMers are allowing customers to get their hands on the technology.

Of the nine allowing public access, a fair smattering are providing it to the Northern Echo, evidently a strong catalyst to encourage public access.

This balance of 10% public access to 90% of authorities using staff as intermediaries is in marked constrast to the developments taking place in university and polytechnic libraries where CD-ROM networks (clusters of terminals linked to a jukebox of CD-ROMs) are seen as an essential means of giving the customers what they want. For a whole variety of reasons we in public libraries are taking a different approach. The case for CD-ROMs as selection/ bibliographic aids is won, the case for purchasing databases to support reference and information services looks set to be a victory, but, perhaps because of the diversity and differing levels of customer ability in public libraries, direct access is not yet seen as the highest priority. We certainly hope that we are not, since it is costly to provide one PC and CD-ROM drive per database and, if there are fewer PCs than databases, switching disks in and out all the time is a pain.

The evidence from the academic sector is that the task is labour intensive and leads to disks 'disappearing'. With the jukebox well out of harm's way and a menu of databases to choose from at the terminal the process is much simplified. The potential of online access is not unlike that of CD-ROM—providing the ability to search very large stores of data—with the added advantage that the information can be as up to date as today.

The risks of incurring high costs through long searches has damped any enthusiasm for providing direct public access to hosts, but online access remains an important tool to those librarians involved in the provision of information services.

Pricing structures which do not discourage the occasional user and the wide availability of microcomputers have seen a steady increase in use over recent years. What used to be a hit-and-miss affair using dedicated terminals and devices called acoustic couplers has become a simple and reliable matter of hitting a few keys. The majority of those libraries who see online searching as an asset to their services have already begun using the technique and that the increases seen in the past are tending to plateau. Whether the remaining 60 authorities suffer a financial barrier, a psychological one or simply do not believe that online searching is relevant to their services cannot be evinced from the data available.

However the nature of the databases most used implies use by libraries who prioritise bibliographic and business information as important. Perhaps the non-users have set other priorities for their services. Modem boards can be fitted into machines and there is bags of cheap software around to be played with. Insofar as online searching can be a suer-friendly business, the micro can facilitate it since it is possible to set up dialling and log-in codes for rapid access, and the micro can still be used for so many other things.

The other significant feature of the data is the steady increase in the number of authorities using the circulation system as the medium of access. While five is a very small figure when compared with the micros, there are some interesting implications in the decision to use the library management system for online searching. First, most of the new systems allow you to do so, and have done for some time.

There is nothing particularly fancy about it, but for very good reasons most libraries have shied away from doing so. While in principle it should be a good thing to provide online access in a variety of locations, where the information is really needed, it requires trained staff to use the systems effectively and untrained staff can run up some hefty bills in no time at all.

Use can be limited to defined terminals, but the strategy which has been to focus online searching to key locations where specialist staff, capable of knowing for certain when online should be used, are on hand. Without doubt, the use of the library management system as a delivery medium holds great potential and we will be very surprised if more libraries do not take the plunge. Certainly if the complexities which remain in host interfaces can be reduced so that infrequent users have a chance of getting in and out more quickly, there is every incentive to widen the network, and that is precisely the value of the library management system has a wide network of terminals.

The truth of these comments becomes more clear when the total terminal population is considered, rather than the use of the medium alone. What we have been looking at so far is the number of authorities using each method, rather than the number of terminals used by each. Just as with the CD-ROM world, we are facing more diversity all the time. While 'umbrella' hosts can give access to a wide range of databases, sometimes duplicating other hosts, there are also individual database providers who are being used by public libraries. The two obvious examples are laser's Viscount inter-lending service and Volnet, which is a database of importance to the voluntary sector. The markets being served by online searching are quite clearly defined and are common to most users.

Blaise is still an important source of bibliographic information, but with a growing range of CD-ROM-based products it may become less used. The major use for online searching is clearly business information. Added together these business-orientated databases dominate Blaise by a factor of more than three to one.

The only joker to be found is Acompline, which is unique in providing current information on local authority affairs and which is still quite popular. The fact that access to this database, which is provided by the London Research Centre, is free may have something to do with this continuing popularity. The CD-ROM/online searching duopoly should be a key focus for our attention over the next few years and will be the subject of further research.

Indeed, a recent report from the Centre for Communication and Information Studies at the Polytechnic of Central London reports research which looked in much more detail at the actual pattern of database use by analysing bills from a range of authorities, and interviewing a sample of users in great detail.

CD-ROMs have been widely seen as a development which widens access to information previously only available through remote online searching systems, by bringing very large databases into a personal computer environment that is easier to use. The advantages of resource sharing which a local network can offer seems to make it an attractive proposition to mount the CD-ROM drives as a network resource which can be accessed from any workstation, to make most effective use of the facility. The majority of CD-ROM networks in the UK are mounted on PC-based local area networks (LANs), since this is the format in which most CD-ROMs are produced. At present the standard available LANs do not properly support the use of CD-ROM, and require the use of third-party software add-ons to manage the optical drives. These are normally controlled by a separate optical file server, a computer adapted with CD controller cards to which the drives are attached.

The advantages of putting CD-ROMs on a network are not only in providing multiple concurrent access to the information, but also in streamlining the actual management of the disks themselves, which would otherwise be distributed and loaded manually. A high level of usage is normally reported by those installing CD networks, and this route offers opportunities for integration of CD databases with other library and information resources, such as online catalogues. A significant level of usage has detrimental effects on the response time, however, and active users are often limited to a small number at one time to maintain a reasonable performance. Since it was originally developed as a single-user device the CD-ROM searching software is not standardized and is not optimized for the management of multiple searches by different users. Large databases which are spread over a number of disks require an equivalent number of drives if the full database is to be networked, or some arrangement for changing the disks.

The newer formats of CD-ROM/XA (Extended Access) and CD-Interactive are not compatible with current network systems, since they require multimedia, capabilities which support the interleaving and synchronisation of data, audio, and graphics. There are three broad alternative architectures for implementing CD-ROMs' on a network, which involve particular decisions on the location of data and program files:

1 A file server arrangement, with the data files located on the file server itself, and the user interface and search engine residing on the client workstation. This leads to a heavy data traffic since entire files must be downloaded to the client before they can be searched, and means that an update to the search software must be done on each of the client workstations.

2 A centralized approach, where both data, search engine and interface are all resident on a multi-user machine, with the workstation acting as a terminal, losing the benefits of peer networking.

3 A client-server approach, where the data files and search engine reside on the server machine, and the user interface with the client workstation. This reduces the communications load by keeping the processing close to the data storage, and enables the full power of the workstation to be available for the client.

This third approach is the subject of current research at Salford University, using the Z39.50 protocol as the basis for communication. A widespread acceptance would require the adoption of one or another standard communication protocol for information retrieval by CD-ROM producers, but would also support the specialisation of individual search engines and user interfaces. At the present time, running CD-ROMs across a local network involves a compromise between all these factors, deriving mainly from the uneasy transition of a device designed principally for single user access into a multi-user environment. The development of the networking environment makes possible other solutions to the information access issue. The decreasing price of data storage makes large databases on a networked hard disk a feasible proposition; and the development of sophisticated user interfaces to remote databases through network gateways makes traditional online searching more approachable for non-expert users.

Electronic Service Delivery

The clutch of technologies which cover electronic information delivery include CDROM, online access to remote database hosts, videotex/teletext and automated community information. They are all well known applications some of which have been around for years—online access must soon be celebrating a quarter of a century of service. That does not mean that every library uses them or that in those that do the systems form a major part of the service.

Public libraries are still very much about lending material for home use—how often are you reference librarians asked whether it is possible to borrow a reference-only item? However, information as a commodity has always been vital to our service and with the growing demands of students and others, it is unlikely to diminish in the near future. If the face of public libraries is to change radically during the next ten years it is probably in the area of electronic information delivery that we will make it happen.

These technologies have literally the potential to give the power of information searching to the customer rather than through the librarian to the customer. That does not mean we are an endangered species if such a situation comes about—the systems will need to be managed, exploited and the customers trained. It does mean that our roles may change. That is the real challenge of electronic information delivery. In the last survey hyperbole was necessary to describe the impact that the CDRom had made on public libraries.

Like the compact disc in the audio market, the CDROM has been the high flier of the late 1980s and will continue to change the way that we operate as librarians (and listeners) well into the 90s. Just to remind you, before looking more closely at the data from the present survey, in 1987 two libraries indicated that they were considering using CDROM while in 1989, 49 were actually in the thick of it. A variety of databases were being used, but all were using Bookbank which was the catalyst for most libraries.

In four years the number has gone up 50 times, since 1989 it has more than doubled. Any way you look at it, CDROM is a popular delivery system for information and is likely to continue its sweep through public libraries. The data are pretty self-evident, there are increases everywhere. Northern Ireland scores a full house while all other authorities show a rapid take-up.

Only Scotland and the Non-Mets lag behind the 60% and over which is seen elsewhere. We commented last time that the size of these two exceptions might create barriers to buying the system and that still seems to be the case; although the relative cheapness of the hardware and the real savings and benefits of using Bookbank, for example, continue to raise question marks about these discrepancies. There are in the end only two possibilities. Either the scale of operations in these two types of authority is such that resources cannot be found for what elsewhere is spreading like wild-fire or, the nature of demand means that other priorities must take precedence.

Looking closely it is not clear that all authorities are using Bookbank, although the vast majority are. Indeed it may well be that those who did not report its use felt that it was not worth mentioning! The data also show, however, that a wide range of databases are now in use, ranging from those of local relevance, such as the Northern Echo, to national newspapers, official publications, British Standards and the odd encyclopedia. Selection tools remain a popular sue for the CDROM equipment and alongside Bookbank we now find Bookfind, American Books in Print, BNB and the British Library Catalogue.

Respondents were asked to indicate whether the systems were staff only or made available directly to the public, without staff intervention. Of the 101 total, 66 indicated that their systems were staff only while nine report direct use by the public. That leaves 26 who said nothing about access. From the databases the 26 'question marks' are using I am pretty sure that they are not providing public access, which means that only about one tenth of CDROMers are allowing customers to get their hands on the technology.

Of the nine allowing public access, a fair smattering (five actually) are providing it to the Northern Echo, evidently a strong catalyst to encourage public access. This balance of 10% public access to 90% of authorities using staff as intermediaries is in marked constrast to the developments taking place in university and polytechnic libraries where CDROM networks are seen as an essential means of giving the customers what they want. For a whole variety of reasons we in public libraries are taking a different approach. The case for CDROMs as selection/bibliographic aids is won, the case for purchasing databases to support reference and information services looks set to be a victory, but, perhaps because of the diversity and differing levels of customer ability in public libraries, direct access is not yet seen as the highest priority.

We certainly hope that we are not, since it is costly to provide one PC and CDROM drive per database and, if there are fewer PCs than databases, switching disks in and out all the time is a pain. The evidence from the academic sector is that the task is labour intensive and leads to disks 'disappearing'. With the jukebox well out of harm's way and a menu of databases to choose from at the terminal the process is much simplified. We are confident that the benefits of direct public access and the provision of networks will appear in the returns when this survey is undertaken again. The breakthrough will come when three criteria can be met.

First, that jukeboxes can be readily connected to the big networks supported by library management systems so that the richness of CDROM databases can be exploited at terminals far and wide. So far, experiments have hit a number of problems of software compatibility and lack of intelligence on the networks and these problems have kept the breakthrough from coming, but come it must.

Second, search software can provide a standard query language which is applicable to all CDROM databases so that the user once trained can sue any system.

And finally, that reasonable pricing structures can be negotiated with CDROM publishers for networking agreements.

Online access to remote database hosts has been around for a long time. It must have been in use outside esoteric research labs for twenty years and many public libraries have been providing online access for upwards of ten. In some ways the potential of online access is not unlike that of CDROM—providing the ability to search very large stores of data—with the added advantage that the information can be as up to date as today.

The risks of incurring high costs through long searches has damped any enthusiasm for providing direct public access to hosts, but online access remains an important tool to those librarians involved in the provision of information services. Pricing structures which do not discourage the occasional user and the wide availability of microcomputers have seen a steady increase in use over recent years. What used to be a hit-and-miss affair using dedicated terminals and devices called acoustic couplers has become a simple and reliable matter of hitting a few keys.

However, we suspect that a continuing subjective feeling that searching online is expensive and complicated has created some barriers and the growing availability of databases on CDROM which incur no cost at point of use has influenced decisions on whether or not to use online searching. There is no conclusive evidence that the two methods overlap significantly, however subjective evidence suggests that an important use of CDROM is the formulation of search strategies which can then be used during an online search. Also, it would appear from a recent report on the 1991 International Online Information Meeting that demand for online hosts continues to grow despite the popularity of CDROM databases.

Turning to the data from this current survey, there are now 107 authorities using online searching. That is a 10% increase over the figure in 1989, which was 97. Looking at the percentage changes since

1985, we can see that there has been a slowing down in the increase—the change between 1985 and 1987 was 30% up, and 1987 to 1989, 13%. This suggests that the majority of those libraries who see online searching as an asset to their services have already begun using the technique and that the increases seen in the past are tending to plateau. Whether the remaining 60 authorities suffer a financial barrier, a psychological one or simply do not believe that online searching is relevant to their services cannot be evinced from the data available.

However, as we shall see below, the nature of the databases most used implies use by libraries who prioritise bibliographic and business information as important. Perhaps the non-users have set other priorities for their services. The fact that only 25% of Scottish authorities use the technique influences significantly the overall total. Non-mets are also at 25% but they are only four in number, yet Scotland, with the largest number of authorities, lags far behind. We cannot claim an in-depth knowledge of Scottish library services, however elsewhere in this review we will see that they tend to plough a separate furrow in their use of IT. The other data show manly steady increases and no decreases, from which we may conclude that once adopted, online searching has lasting value to service delivery. A trend which previously proved of interest is the method of access used to search online hosts. Trend is an important word in this context since, on occasion, the replies received from the questionnaire needed some interpretation. When compared with 1985, the data from the current survey reinforce patterns which were noted in 1989. The fairly even mix of dedicated terminal, Prestel and microcomputer which existed in 1985 has been routed by the micro which now stands head, shoulders and keyboard above all other access methods. Not really very surprising when you come to think about it since the micro has been widely adopted as the access medium for those who operate outside our world.

Modem boards can be fitted into machines and there is bags of cheap software around to be played with. Insofar as online searching can be a suer-friendly business, the micro can facilitate it since it is possible to set up dialling and log-in codes for rapid access, and the micro can still be used for so many other things. The other significant feature of the data iis the steady increase in the number of authorities using the circulation system as the medium of access.

While five is a very small figure when compared with the micros, there are some interesting implications in the decision to use the library management system for online searching. First, most of the new systems allow you to do so, and have done for some time. There is nothing particularly fancy about it, but for very good reasons most libraries have shied away from doing so. While in principle it should be a good thing to provide online access in a variety of locations, where the information is really needed, it requires trained staff to use the systems effectively and untrained staff can run up some hefty bills in no time at all.

Use can be limited to defined terminals, but the strategy which has been to focus online searching to key locations where specialist staff, capable of knowing for certain when online should be used, are on hand. Without doubt, the use of the library management system as a delivery medium holds great potential and we will be very surprised if more libraries do not take the plunge (or the risk?). Certainly if the complexities which remain in host interfaces can be reduced so that infrequent users have a chance of getting in and out more quickly, there is every incentive to widen the network, and that is precisely the value of the library management system 0 it has a wide network of terminals.

The truth of these comments becomes more clear when the total terminal population is considered, rather than the use of the medium alone. What we have been looking at so far is the number of authorities using each method, rather than the number of terminals used by each.

	1989	1991
Dedicated terminal	45	68
Circulation system	35	61
Microcomputer	121	263
Prestel, etc.	4	2

There can be no certainty about the freedom which is allowed for all of the library management system terminals to be used for on line searching, but the potential is clear. Other points to note from these data are that although the number of dedicated terminal users has risen by only one in two years, there has been a 50% increase in the terminals in use; suggesting that while this route may not be the one chosen now by new entries, for those already using the method, it is of sufficient value to encourage wider availability. If these data are considered in conjunction with the 'other' category, the trend in the use of online searching is quite apparent.

Blaise is still an important source of bibliographic information, but with a growing range of CDROM-based products it may become less used. The major use for online searching is clearly business information. Added together these business-orientated databases dominate Blaise by a factor of more than three to one. The only joker to be found is Acompline, which is unique in providing current information on local authority affairs and which is still quite popular. The fact that access to this database, which is provided by the London Research Centre, is free may have something to do with this continuing popularity.

The last two aspects of online searching which can be considered here relate not to the technology or the range of services available, but how they are delivered to users. The first factor is the costs which are passed on to users and the second is the management of the service—staff skilled in the techniques and how it has changed traditional provision. Charging policies ought to tell us a great deal about the priorities of libraries and their responses to changes especially those outside their control, whether from competition or from the comments of the Minister for the Arts!

Back in 1989 made some observations about the reasons for the high level of certain replies. Discretion, for example, could be an excuse for saying one thing and doing another—telling everyone that certain categories of user are charged, or charges are levied when a search is requested, while not bothering because of the hassle of recovering the money. No comment, on the other hand could be an excuse for doing almost anything; anything that is except charge.

The use of online searching has grown up in a tradition where it is the exception to levy a fee for a service at point of use. The whole point of public goods is that they are funded from individual contributions (rates, taxes) which bear no relation to level of use made by that individual. The management of the service includes the organisation of specialist staff and the changes which have resulted from the development of online searching. There is just as much need to have highly trained staff undertaking searches as there has ever been.

Despite developments in the design of user-friendly interfaces, online searching remains a special skill, both in the knowledge of command languages and in the formulation of suitable search strategies. It is likely to be a long time before access is provided to customers without the need for a trained intermediary, since cost rises and effectiveness falls if the searcher is not properly trained. Libraries were asked to indicate numbers of locations of trained staff and 86 provided replies, as opposed to 78 in 1989. As with all questions demanding more than a yes or no reply, we must be cautious about making too many assumptions from the data.

The evidence provided in the replies shows that all but a very few authorities focus their online services (and staff) in key locations—usually reference libraries, business information centres and the like. The average number of trained staff in each authority is something over four, a slight increase on 1989, but remains fairly stable. It seems that whatever changes may face public libraries in the next few years, this is at least one service which will continue to require 'gatekeepers' to make it fully effective.

Changes in the form of other services resulting from the use of online searching was the last question asked on this subject. Again, since the data re textual rather than precise responses, only general conclusions may be drawn. Despite that, the replies add some detail to the overall picture of online searching in public libraries. Fifty seven authorities commented, compared with the 39 who did so in 1989. Of those 28 implied in their reply that online searching had enriched the range of services available.

Eight libraries reported that printed sources had been cancelled and ten that there had been no significant change; either because online had been used for so long that no-one could remember what life was like before, or online was such a new acquisition that there had not been time to see any impact. On the other hand, two authorities reported dramatic changes to the scope and method of service delivery. While online searching involves only a few staff and demands small amounts of the budget, it is an important and emotive topic.

The trend which has emerged over the past four or five years is for the databases to form part of services to business and now, for those services to be viewed in many places as 'suitable cases for charging'. The CDROM/online searching duopoly should be a key focus for our attention over the next few years and will, I am sure, be the subject of further research. Indeed, a recent report from the Centre for Communication and Information Studies at the Polytechnic of Central London reports research which looked in much more detail at the actual pattern of database use by analyzing bills from a range of authorities, and interviewing a sample of users in great detail.

The general trends reported above are echoed in the research results and the report is well worth reading to gain a clearer picture of what the future may hold. We cannot end this section without saying something about LANet since Email is just a special sort of online searching. We suggested that is most public libraries used LANet regularly, it might be used as a medium to distribute the results of this survey.

There are now more on the network, it has not become an important element in the pattern of our communications. What is puzzling is the fact that the academic network JANET is widely used by university and polytechnic libraries and librarians to talk to each other.

By and large, through this survey until now we have seen a mixture of steady growth in some applications, dramatic growth in others. Turning now to videotex and teletext we are in the realm of technologies which have been around for some years, have become well established, to the point where we are beginning to see them superseded. We can remember a time when there was much talk about Prestel (videotex) as a major medium of information delivery.

Organisations were clamouring to be a part of a readily accessible and widely spread public network. Today Prestel is still around, but many new systems have arrived which are Prestel-like in their utility, but have much more power to exploit data resources. Such systems are now used in private viewdata networks, closed user group systems providing information using the format of Prestel, but managed by some local information provider.

Teletext, an information system available on broadcast television networks such as Ceefax and Oracle has never been a critical element in publicly provided information services since the data cannot be manipulated locally and is usually of momentary interest—news, racing results, etc. Moreover, it is common for home use television sets to be sold with Ceefax and Oracle decoders as standard. The trends for teletext and videotex show a situation which has matured to the point where use has levelled off and appears at present to be falling slightly.

Private viewdata, on the other hand, is growing steadily in popularity as a medium for the delivery of information tailored to the local community. In six years there has been an almost threefold increase in the systems in use and we may expect this to continue since often these systems are developed as corporate information systems, sometimes managed by the library service, sometimes not and while libraries may find themselves low down on the corporate IT programme private viewdata systems may not.

Analysing use at the level of the authority provides only a general picture of developments and that to establish more clearly the impact made it is necessary to consider the penetration of systems within individual authorities. Respondents were asked to report the numbers of terminals used on each of these systems and, in addition, to show whether their use was seldom, steady or constant. These data support earlier points about the fall in the popularity of videotex and teletext as information systems in libraries.

Not only has there been a fall in the number of authorities using the systems, but the number of terminals provided has also dropped—videotex almost to the level of 1985, teletext below it. Of course, mean numbers are just that, and the actual distribution shows that in a few authorities there are relatively large populations of terminals. Wiltshire, for example, reports 38 for videotex. In contrast, not only has the total number of authorities using private viewdata risen, but the mean number of terminals shows a 23.5% rise.

Not surprising since if private viewdata is the means of delivering community information, as it usually is, then terminals should be as widely available as possible. Having descended from the level of total use, to penetration within a library system, we can finally consider how much the systems are used. The questionnaire invited comment on whether the use of each of the three system was seldom, steady or, constant. We must exercise some caution. One person's steady is another's constant and we can only draw limited information from these data. Also, use is likely to vary from terminal to terminal so the single comment may not reflect reality where more than one is in use. Steady is the most frequently cited option, except for videotex where seldom is top. We do not think there is much value in a detailed analysis of these data since their objectivity is questionable, but we can give a personal opinion.

Videotex is not used much since alternative sources of information may provide speedier access (and you have to pay to use Prestel). The cost of teletext is unaffected by use since it is broadcast with the TV signals. Leaving terminals lying about for people to play with, therefore carries no risk of large bills. Safe for the customer to come in and tinker with.

The automation of community information highlights one of the paradoxes of information technology. It is very easy to start—just buy a micro and printer, some database software and off you go—but it can be very hard to keep the data comprehensive and up to date. Anyone who has had much to do with computers knows that the data are the most valuable commodity, much more valuable than the hardware or software that can be replaced at the corner shop. Creating any database takes time, maintaining it takes time, and time is money. Community information has always been an attractive product to automate since so much of it is in the form that can readily be fitted into database software products. Clubs, societies, business organisations and the like are the lifeblood of the community information database and are maintained in some form or other by the vast majority of libraries.

Indeed, comprehensive community systems are something unique to libraries; you certainly can't buy them at Smiths. Not surprisingly then the number of libraries automating community information continues to grow. 1987 and 1989 has been matched in the past two years by a total increase of just over 19%. the rend which was apparent between 1985 and 1987, use of the micro and wordprocessor, has now changed. This time the micro, still the most popular medium, remains unchanged at 38 while use of the library management system shows the most significant growth, up by 75%. It is also not unexpected that private viewdata continues to increase since we have already noted in this chapter that the number of authorities providing the medium continues to rise. One question which comes immediately to mind, however, is if 40 authorities reported use of the system under the videotex/teletext section above, but only 18 report using it for community information, what are the other 22 doing? Just the same question had to be asked in the last survey and suggested that the problem was one of interpretation—that the authorities might not be managing the private viewdata system and therefore thought that it should not be reported under the community information banner.

The prime purpose of private viewdata networks is to deliver information of relevance to the community. Finally, while considering the method of processing, it should be noted that a further five libraries indicated that they were actively investigating the automation on their community information files, and by now they may have done just that. That gives a potential total of 102 authorities who use IT for community information or 60% of the 167 country wide. Micros and wordprocessors have been around for so many years, have at least 40% of the libraries in the country not started to automate the community information files which they certainly must have.

With common sense, transferring manual files to a micro can save time and make the product much more useful. Mail merge makes remainders easier and with multiple indexing possible, more variety of presentation is not a problem. A micro/printer set up is not pricey and there are so many examples of applications that not to try seems swimming against the stream. To see whether there was any pattern to this reticence we looked a bit more closely at the 66 libraries without automated community information. An interesting fact emerged—that nearly half of the 66 were authorities of the same type. Twenty seven of the 41 Scottish authorities (66%) have yet to do anything about automating their community information; only one of the four Welsh Non-Mets has done so and none of the Northern Ireland libraries has started.

Elsewhere, the most likely authority type to find automated systems is the English county where 85% have automated their community information. London, the Mets and the Welsh counties range from 74% uptake down to 63%. You will remember that Scottish authorities were also behind on the library management system front and one can only repeat that perhaps they have set different priorities or lack of resources places severe restrictions on the acquisition of technology. Conversely, English counties are large organisations with disparate service points and the benefits of using IT for community information has clearly been recognised.

5

Management of Automated Libraries

In a changing world, librarians have a responsibility not only to know about the ways in which libraries can use the techniques of automation, but also to be aware of the changes automation can bring to library service in the near and perhaps the more distant future. It is easy in this twentieth century to strive for change simply for its own sake, just as it is even easier to strive for retaining the status quo. Those librarians whose task it is to decide for or against the particular change of automation need especially of be on their guard against these two attitudes. They need to make their decisions in the light of facts; facts about their libraries as they are now; what services are provided to what people by what library staff and at what cost, and similar facts about any proposed system of library automation. In this a library is no different from any other office or factory considering the use of a computer to perform a given job of work most economically. Where the difference does arise, however, is in the concept of a library's service. A factory may charge a certain price for its products and so, hopefully, make an overall profit on its operations. In such circumstances a computer can be shown to act either to increase or to reduce profits.

But there are few libraries today which exist in order to make a profit for their owners, and few are required to balance an income from subscriptions against their expenses. How, then, can a price be set against the service which a library can provide, and how can this price be measured so that automation may be seen to be justified? An answer to these questions can be found in two ways. Firstly, any industrial librarian knows that his job is to satisfy his company's information needs. He, a specialist in information work, can supply information to company employees more efficiently than they can obtain it themselves, and so the value of his library's service can be expressed in terms of minutes and hours of saved time, and hence in monetary terms. An analogous argument can be used of the reader service functions in university and public libraries. Secondly, the value of a library's service can also be expressed quantitatively in terms of the chief librarian's bargaining power at meetings of the library committee, and so in terms of the hard cash voted to him to enable him to run his library.

To express the value of automated library systems in quantitative terms and so to compare an automated library with its conventional counterpart. The decision to automate or not to automate can then be taken in the full light of the facts. That this decision seems frequently to have been taken in ignorance of the facts does not invalidate the argument, nut serves merely to throw into clearer relief the well-known truths that librarians are, as a class, busy, that libraries struggle for enough money to buy all the books they want, let alone finance a proper automation feasibility study, and that it is much easier to obtain money to buy computer equipment than to buy books.

Furthermore, once the computer is working in the library it is seldom difficult to show that improved standards of service have resulted, even though it has probably not been possible to reduce the staff required, and even though the library's total overall expenditure will almost certainly have risen.Final situation in most cases will be that improved library service has been bought at a price. If the librarian has been able to justify this to has committee, then, according to our argument, the automated system has at least "broken even".

We must look a little more closely into the reasons why a librarian might consider using a computer in his library in order to improve its working in some way. And the first kind of reason, which we shall term emotional, is one unfortunate outcome of the automation revolution through which the advanced nations of the world are now passing. According to the emotional argument, computers are modern and efficient, a library which uses a computer in some way must necessarily also be efficient and forward-looking, and almost certainly therefore a good library. It is indeed true to say that those libraries which have introduced computer systems are modern and forward-looking.

The automated systems may well be efficient and the library may be a good one. But it is certainly not necessarily true to say, as the emotional argument does, that if a library uses a computer then it will be all these things. That this reason exists at all, even if only as an attitude of mind, is a direct result of the false glamour ascribed to the computer and the shallow thinking and writing of those responsible for automating aspects of library routines. If, as seems likely, computers will fill a necessary role in libraries in the future, now is indeed the time for some libraries to experiment with ways and means of enabling computers to take their proper place in library work. These experiments should yield both qualitative and quantitative results. Computer is an electronic machine for manipulating symbols. For out purposes, we can readily make this definition more meaningful if we say that a computer can be regarded in many ways as being like a clerk. And if it is a clerk, then we may be able to use it to do clerical work in libraries more quickly, accurately, and more efficiently than it is done at present.

It might even be possible to teach it some professional or intellectual jobs. Being a machine it should not tire under heavy work loads, and in fact, should become more efficient as the work load increases so that as library grows this can be accommodated without proportionate increases in staff. From what we know about computer applications in other fields, we should expect automation to be feasible only in larger libraries or in cases where a number of smaller libraries combine together to form one large unit for processing purposes.

Growth of on-line techniques, which are particularly suited to some areas of library work, will make it realistic for libraries to expect to have on-line access to a large and powerful machine, rather than consider purchasing a small machine for their own use. We are now witnessing the gradual birth of widespread co-operation among libraries, founded upon the fact that modern techniques of electronic data storage, processing, and transmission make possible the speedy and accurate exchange of bibliographic date.

New concepts of bibliographic control and library service are emerging as a direct result of computer applications to library work. A well-established set of procedures exists, leading from the point we have now reached, that of having stated in general terms the advantages which might be expected to accrue from using a computer, to that of installing, testing, and running an automated system in a library. To follow all these procedures faithfully might seem pedantic, perhaps unnecessary in many circumstances, but it is necessary if the job is to be done honestly, avoiding emotion, cultivating reason, and working in quantitative terms.

Because procedures will be enumerated and discussed in one particular way, it does not mean that this is the only way, or that different combinations and distributions of these procedures might not result in very different patterns of overall working; only that the basic ideas must follow one another in this way. The first step towards introducing an automated system is to carry out a feasibility study. This may be done at any level of detail, but the purpose is to ascertain whether or not a computer can be used to do a particular job more efficiently than heretofore. It can be an expansive stage, and may be broken down into two parts, the first one to ascertain if the feasibility study itself is worth undertaking. It is common knowledge that many such studies have shown that a computer was not ledge that many such studies have shown that a computer was not really needed at all, and that the information gained from the feasibility study was sufficient to improve the existing system so as to make it more efficient than the automated one first contemplated.

It is during the feasibility study that systems analysis takes place. The system, be it the whole library itself or only one department, is analysed; its method of working is systematically taken apart piece by piece, so that in the end all the pieces are known and understood, as are the ways in which they fit together to make the whole. If only one department of the library is being investigated, the relationships between it and the other departments, and the library itself, must also be known and understood. Measurement will also take place so that the final result of the study can be in quantitative terms. Numbers will be counted; the numbers of items bought, catalogued, lost, circulated, damaged, and the way these number may be expected to change in the future will be discovered. Also counted will be the number of people needed to do the various jobs in the system, and the time to do each jobs in the system, and the time to do each job will be measured.

The end results of all this library activity be calculated or estimated. This can be difficult because it is not easy to apply a measure to a student reading a book, a chemist pleased with a morsel of information, or a housewife experimenting with new dishes described in a cookery book borrowed from her local public library. It must be attempted, however, because any automated system is likely to alter the pattern of service offered by the library, and this is as important in the final evaluation as the numbers of books ordered each week, or the time it takes to discharge an overdue book.

From all these measurements the costs of the present system will be calculated. They will almost certainly be expressed as unit costs—the cost of cataloguing the "average" book, or answering the "typical" reference question. Together with details of the services performed by the present system and in particular any difficulties and problems associated with it, any aspects which are like to become unsatisfactory in the light of future developments will be indicated, and all will be used by management to make an educated decision about the introduction of automation.

Because the introduction of computerised operations is not the only, and not necessarily the best solution to the problems that will have been brought to light, the next stage of the study is just to find the best solution, automated or not. It is highly desirable, therefore, that the study should be carried out by persons who have no direct interests in seeing that a computer system is installed, perhaps even using a particular make of computer. They should be perfectly free to advise on the optimal course of action.

Like wise, the investigators should have considerable experience of similar studies, and be well informed on all data processing and work study techniques. Needless to say there is a great shortage of such people. Feasibility studies, therefore, are not cheap and so are often skimped or omitted entirely. If the introduction of automation is indicated, and this is the only case that really concerns us here, then the second stage of the study will involve the selection of a computer and the various necessary ancillary items of equipment and stationery needed by the system.

There are considerable differences between the different makes and metals of computer on the market, so that the selection of the machine most suited to the purpose on hand will have a marked effect on the final operating efficiency of the system. The end result of this second stage of the study is a broad system specification. It will indicate the hardware or machinery required and, in general terms, how everything will work.

The throughput or work load handled will be given, as will the estimated costs. Staffing requirements will almost certainly be different from those of the old system, for keypunchers will replace clerks and it will be necessary to have a senior staff member, with data processing experience, in charge of operations and one or two programmes may be required on a permanent basis. Staff requirements will be very different where a library installs a computer for its own use, from the case where it merely uses a short time each week or someone else's machine. Because computers work in ways radically different from human beings, the flow of work in an automated system can differ quite considerably from that in the corresponding manual system.

Old departmental barriers can therefore be broken down of the introduction of automation, as similar processes in different departments are combined and as duplication of work is eliminated. The overall organisational structures of the library can be materially altered, and this will be appreciated and stated in the feasibility study. Once an automated system is considered in any detail it is apparent that it offers a range of possible products and services considerable winter than does a conventional system. The compilation of all kinds of statistics is but one example of this.

A library can expect, therefore, to expand the scope of its operations by introducing mechanised routines, and it is desirable either that the team doing the study include a good knowledge of library service among their skills, or that one member of the library staff work closely with the team, in order that the full possibilities of winter operations are realised. Only in the largest libraries would a feasibility study be likely to indicate clear overall cost reductions through introducing automated methods.

In other libraries the situation would almost certainly be that at the present time a computer-aided system would cost more but would bring additional advantages. It is up to the management to decide whether these advantages justify the increased costs, bearing in mind that, in time, costs will tend to change in favour of automation. If we assume that a decision is made in favour of automation, where does the library go from here? The answer is that the next stages in this idealised introduction of mechanisation will depend very considerably on the extent of the automation which is planned, on the organisational framework of which the library is a part, and no what we can term the library's computing environment. The procedures for implementing an automated circulation system, for example, will be different from those required by a system embracing all a library's technical processing routines. In a university environment the library would expect to make use of a central university computing facility rather than purchase its own machine or use the services of a commercial bureau. This will affect not only the type of machine used, which is likely to be better suited to mathematical than to library work, and the languages programs are written in, but also, because programming may well be done in the computing laboratory, it will affect the staffing requirements in the library.

The overall computing policy of the organisation of which any library is a part will also affect such factors as, for example, the frequency with which computer runs can be made, or whether on-line working is, or is planned to be, available, and so be an important factor in the design of the library system. In large organisations it not infrequently happens that a library in another division or department has already automated some of its functions. It may be possible to take these programs over just as they stand or with only small modifications. In the majority of instances, however, the library's computer system will have to be created from scratch. This stage—system design—can be regarded as consisting of two main parts, although in practice they can so merge together as to be indistinguishable. The first part involves floe-charting the ways in which the system will work, and then in more detail, the several operations and decisions performed by the computer in working the system. The second part, which is the job of programming, carries on in more detail and converts the flow charts into a sequence of computer instructions—a program. It is quite possible for one person, or one group of persons, to carry out both of these two steps, in which case the distinction between them is obscured. Alternatively, the second step, which has more of the character of straight forward routine than the first, can be performed by a programmer.

In either case it is absolutely vital that at the stage of system design proper all the implications for the library of the various detailed decisions and operations which will be included in the final program are fully understood. This requirement can be achieved, as during the feasibility study, by having as senior library staff member work with the system design group, but, ideally, the system designer or designers should themselves be experienced librarians. Similarly, it is best for the programming to be done by someone with a good knowledge of librarianship. Here, however, we come face to face with some very real problems associated with the fact that this whole subject of automation in libraries is a relationship between two disciplines.

Few people, even nowadays when their great worth is appreciated, are at the same time experienced librarians and knowledgeable and up to date in computing matters. If it is vital that an automated library system be designed with all its implications for librarianship in mind, it is, at the very least, highly desirable that the programs are written so as to make the system as efficient as possible from a computing point of view. So library systems are very often designed as a co-operative venture between library and computing department staff in order to assemble together the necessary skills and expertise.

The work is often done as a sideline, or even in staffs' own time. That so much sound work has been more rapid and more quantitative analyses made had these methods of working been less common. Where it is difficult to find the time to design and implement automated system, the detailed analyses and comparisons necessary for its full justification and evaluation naturally tend to be skimped or omitted. Overall impressions are substituted and, as a result, the library profession wherein the arguments of emotion can flourish. The languages in which computer programs for library routines are written are important subjects for discussion at the present time. For mathematical, commercial, and other special kinds of work, a number of high-level programming languages have been defined. These make it easy for the programmer because the programming language can be quite similar in form and content to the language ordinarily used in the particular discipline. The price paid for this programming facility is a less efficient use of machine time. This is unimportant in one-off jobs, but it becomes a major factor in library systems where a program is run frequently.

A further advantage of high-level languages is that they can often be run on many different makes and types of computer; on all machines, in fact, for which a special translating or compiler program has been written. This takes each instruction in the high-level language and converts it into the necessary number of detailed machine instructions for the computer concerned. Programs written in high-level languages can thus be exchanged widely, to the overall conservation of programming manpower. Because of the machine inefficiency of high-level languages, library programs tend to be written in what are termed low-level languages. These make better use of computer time but, being less similar to natural language and requiring the use of quite detailed instructions, make greater demands on the programmer's time and ability. They are generally applicable to only make or series of computers, and so do not permit free exchange and utilisation of programs. In a situation where computing power is at a premium, library programs will tend to be written in low-level languages at the expense of programming manpower.

Where programming manpower is at a premium, the tendency will be to use high-level languages at the expense of computing power. Present trends are beginning to indicate that, in future, library programs will be written in high-level languages and exchanged freely in order to save the very considerable effort which would be entailed were each library top design and program its own systems. When a program, has finally been written, it must then be tested, or "de-bugged", to remove as many as possible of the errors which the fallible human system-designers and programmers will have written into it. This is generally done by running the programs with test date to simulate as many as possible of the circumstances that are likely to arise in real-life working. It is at this stage that the value of an experienced programmer is most apparent. He will have written fewer errors into the program to start with and will be able to discover more readily why things go wrong when they do, and be able to put them right.

Programming skill in this respect is particularly valuable when working with low-level languages. After this stage the program is ready to being work with real library data, nut it is usual to place one more safeguard against error in the machine system by working the new system in parallel with the old for a few months. After this period, if everything is satisfactory, the support provided by the old system in event of failure of the new is removed and the automated system, having been thoroughly tried, takes over full responsibility. Machines, of course, like human beings, are not infallible and they do from time to time make mistakes or break down. A safety net must therefore be provided so that in the event of machine failure no data is lost and the system can carry on, or safely suspend operations until the failure can be rectified. Such a safely suspend operations until the failure can be rectified. Such a safety net can be provide with a coarse or with a fine mesh, the latter being more expensive.

A coarse-meshed net, commonly termed a fail soft sub-system, permits only limited degree of confusion and disruption of operations to result from machine failure. A net with fine mesh, a fail safe sub-system, constitutes an analogous set of producers with allow operations to continue normally with, hopefully, no confusion. The sort of net employed in each situation will be determined by the importance of the particular system and the value to be placed on keeping the relevant records intact. For example, a library could not possibly allow any of its shelf list records to be accidentally destroyed, while it would be of little consequence if overdue letters for student book loans were not sent because of machine failure. Once an automated library system is working satisfactorily, it becomes important that it should continue to do so. Procedures in the event of machine failure are only one aspect of this general problem.

Equally important is the need to establish a good working relationship between the library and the computing department so that the desired standard of library service is maintained. A library system usually demands that a computer run be made at a stated time each day, week, or month. For example, where a university library has introduced a computerised circulation system, it is necessary that an updated printout of books on loan should be available in the circulation department each day. If anything cases this printout to be delayed, then the work of the circulation department will be hindered. In fact, in the case of circulation control it is true to say that the whole justification of an automated system hinges on the daily printout being available at the right time each day.

Library work must often therefore receive high priority in the computing department, and this can be difficult to achieve. In some organisations, however, computing policy, and thus the order of priority of the different users, is determined by a special computing committee and not by the head of the computing department. If the library can put a sufficiently strong case to such a committee, then the necessary degree of priority will be guaranteed and, consequently, the desired quality of library service ensured. In some instances the first move towards library automation comes from within the computing department, and then this difficulty should not arise if the importance of priorities is emphasised by the librarian from the early stages of the project.

The correct note will be sounded, if, instead of speaking simply about "changes" in computer science, we use the word "improvement" and say that improvement are continually and very rapidly being made to computers and the ways in which they can be used. This it is certain that within a few years of introducing a particular automated system, improvements in computers will make it possible to re-design the system for a more modern machine so as to extend the scope of what is being done and to do it more cheaply. Of course it may well happen that the particular computer used by the library will not have been replaced so quickly and improvements which would be made possible by a newer machine cannot be made. It is unusual for a given computer to remain in service for more than 10 years, and after 5 years newer machines will being to make a change very desirable. The implications for libraries of this state of flux are very considerable, especially since, until recently, libraries have exhibited only a very slow rate of change. Librarians, despite or perhaps because of the conservations they display in relation to changes in libraries, show a remarkable interest in the very latest computing techniques that are either still in the early experimental stages or no more than ideas in designers' brains.

These future developments invariably hold out the promise of solving all the world's problems of bibliographic organisation, and, perhaps not unnaturally, librarians grasp eagerly at them. But when the full implications of such developments are pointed out in terms of the sacrifices and changes each library would have to make in order to adopt them, then the former panacea can become less attractive. Once a program has been implemented in a library it will not be long before the need will become apparent to make small additions and changes to it. These must be done by a programmer and will sometimes involve considerable alterations in the whole structure of the program.

Where automation in a library has progressed beyond an elementary stage, it will become very desirable for the library to have a programmer on its permanent staff and perhaps a more senior person, a systems analyst, as well. An embryonic data processing department will have been created within the library because of this requirement for constant minor change and improvement. It will have responsibilities in all the conventional library departments where automated routines have been introduced and must have the authority to see that any changes are made in such a way that they satisfy the requirements of efficiency laid down for the system itself.

Once such as department of data processing has been established, a library will be in a good position to keep abreast of advance in computer science and will be able to modify the library's own systems from time to time to take fullest advantage of changes in the facilities offered in the computing unit where the library's work is done. Being actually on the library's own permanent staff, members of the library data processing department will be able to take full account of the librarianship aspects of their work. This is the ideal situation, and where a library is introducing automation on anything more than a very limited scale, the establishment of such a department should be given high priority.

In order to complete this picture of libraries and automation it is necessary to try to look a short distance into the future, to see what development are likely to come about in computing and how libraries will be able to use them.

Because of the rapid rate of change in the field of automations, such future knowledge becomes essential if one is fully to understand the present situation and to know how to plan for library systems which will become operational in a few years' time. There is one fairly recent development in this which should be of the greatest importance in the future. In Britain, there now exist a number of working parties, each active in some areas of the field of library automation. Each owes its existence to the fact that a number of library automation. Each owes its existence to the fact that a number of libraries are co-operating and pooling their resources to speed progress. Some of the working parties are designing systems for a particular make of computer, while others have no such limitation.

Some are concentrating on the problems of one particular type of library, while others consider all types of library. It is beginning to seem likely that when these groups finally produce viable systems each will be adopted with little or no change by several libraries. One group in particular is designing a book-ordering system in such a way that it includes most of the features required by libraries and can readily be altered to cater for special individual preferences. This co-operation will be of the greatest importance in future. Now, and always, it makes possible savings in programming effort and speeds the introduction of automation where this has been shown to be justified.

When cataloguing data in machineable from become more generally available, for example, its use by individual libraries will be facilitated where numbers of libraries are using identical or similar cataloguing systems. The situation will be similar where a new technique or piece of equipment becomes available to a group of libraries which are using one type of computer.

A new improved program need be written once only to be capable of adoption by all members of the group. Once a group of libraries have automated all or some of their activities and have proved this to be an advantage, other libraries will find it to their advantage either to adopt the common systems as they stand or with the minimum possible alterations. Among university libraries at least, programs will be made available freely. It is much easier to talk of library co-operation in this way then to achieve it in practice. Although all libraries are the same to the extent that they buy, catalogue, store, and lend books and other material, they do differ considerably in that they buy different kinds of books, catalogue them in different ways, and serve many different types of readers. Accordingly, libraries have developed in many different ways, and rightly so.

But it is nonetheless true that when comparing the various methods of performing a given job, the differences tend to be in matters of detail, and that underneath is a large area of common practice. This makes it reasonable to expect that co-operating libraries will be able to accept large segments of automated systems as they stand and will need to later only details. It is true that some apparently trivial differences in points of detail can make the adoption of a whole system impossible, but such cases are the exception rather than the rule. There is a very broad spectrum of different types of library, each with different needs, but it should be possible for the whole spectrum of needs to be satisfied by there or four major types of automated system. Three such divisions of the spectrum of libraries might be as follows:

1) *Small libraries*, having simple cataloguing needs and buying straightforward material from limited number of suppliers.

2) *Medium and large libraries*, buying a wide range of materials from all parts of the world, with cataloguing needs more complex than type (1) but not so demanding as (2). Full control of circulations needed and individual treatment,

particularly as regards cataloguing, is required for special collections.

3) *National and other very large libraries* with complex acquisition procedures for all types of library materials. Fully detailed cataloguing is necessary for very large catalogues which may have to be related to the production of a national bibliography.

Standardisation tendency is to be observed in most aspects of life today. Its advantage is to be found in the reduction of costs it makes possible. Despite our understandable attachment to our differences, we accept standardisation because of the clear advantages it offers. A good illustration for our purpose can be seen in the motor industry. People's transport need tend to fall into a small number of well-defined classes, and so do the types of motor car that are produced.

A fair amount of individual differences in needs and preferences are catered for by different manufactures and by the addition of optional extras and preferences can be catered for by adding "optional extras" to the above three design types, and further variety will be ensured by the fact that differing systems will be produced by the various working parties. These universal schemes are with us already and, despite their acknowledged short-comings, libraries have already begun to change over to using them.

The advantages to be gained from a central source are considered to make worthwhile the very great task of conversion involved, for example, in reclassifying a library's whole collection. The greatest pressures towards standardisation will come in this area of cataloguing as a result of advances in the practice of librarianship that are associated with the introduction of automation. Three events are combining together at the present time which are potentially capable of effecting very great changes in library practice throughout the world. Firstly, the Library of Congress Shared Cataloguing Program is extending the scope of the Library of Congress printed catalogue card service to include all material from western European countries. Secondly, the introduction of standard book numbering in Britain, besides facilitating the acquisition of books by libraries, provides a unique tag for each book which can readily be handled by computer, and enables cataloguing copy for new books to be recorded by the British National Bibliography from 3 to 6 weeks before publication. If standard book numbering is adopted by other countries, and there is good reason to hope that it will, be then the cataloguing copy provided by the Library of Congress shared Cataloguing Program will also be available a similar period before publication. The third event, or rather programme of events, is the Library of Congress MARC (Machine-Readable Cataloguing) Project. When this has been fully implemented it will make the cataloguing copy, collected in advance of publication by the Shared Cataloguing Program, available to libraries in machineable form. The format of these machineable catalogue records is designed to facilitate the exchange of cataloguing copy between libraries and to enable individual libraries to modify and adapt the records to their own particular needs. Such modification can be of two kinds, programmable and non-programmable.

Programmable alterations can be performed automatically by the computer when the machineable catalogue record is added to the library's own internal records. They included standard abbreviating operations on headings, descriptions, and classification number, and the reformatting of entries.

The basic idea behind such programmable alternations is that they are standard. Non-programmable alterations involve human intervention and are needed whenever part of a catalogue record must be changed to some form that cannot be derived by algorithm from the original record. All such alterations cost money and the non-programmable ones will be the more expensive of the two kinds. Centrally produced cataloguing copy, of course, has been with us for some time, and it has been bought by many libraries, especially in the United States. Two drawbacks have prevented its more wide-spread use; the comparative slowness of the service and the low percentage of libraries' total acquisitions covered. Both these disadvantages should expect to have approximately 70-80 per cent of their new acquisition covered by the Library of Congress service. Librarians have long realised the advantages of central cataloguing service and have been aware of the great waste of effort when books are catalogued in each library where copies are bought. Now it is likely that this long-standing dream will soon materialise.

Another librarians' drams may also be realised over the next few decades as a result of this co-operation in cataloguing: the national catalogue given the holdings of all libraries in the country and also containing entries for all new books as they are published, able to be searched by computer from remote on-line terminals, appears to librarians to solve very many of the problems that they have today. There are very great obstacles of the problems that they have today.

There are very great obstacles to be overcome before such a catalogue can be made a reality, but work being done now leads one to expect that it will eventually come to exist. Machineable copy for all new books it almost with us and the investigations now in progress 9 on how to convert the entries in the British Museum catalogue to machineable from should enable a very large corpus of existing catalogue material to be included in the national catalogue.

The very real difficulties in programming a machine catalogue search by author and title, cased by inconsistencies in cataloguing, can be overcome by standard book numbers for new books and for old ones. Direct access computer memories are rapidly increasing in size and should cause no serious problems. Advantages of such a catalogue are considerable. Primarily, it will give the locations of material listed in it and remove almost all the inefficiency and frustration from existing systems of inter-library lending. As such, it will be a major adjunct to national scholarship.

Libraries will be able to extract cataloguing data for new acquisitions directly from it by means of on-line consoles. This act will automatically indicate a location in that library for the items concerned. Local catalogues, whether printed on paper or kept only in machine memory, will list the most frequently used material only. Thus, great savings will be realised in catalogue printing costs or in machine memory storage devoted permanently to library catalogues. Uniformity in cataloguing practice will be further encourage. Libraries' dreams of the future begin to bring the handling of textual material within the scope of systems of automation.

Facsimile transmission of photographs is an everyday occurrence in the newspaper industry where speed is all important and where the volume of information is comparatively small. Transmission of printed pages by these means is practicable and economical over short distances where there is a high traffic density, but up to the present there has been little demand from libraries for higher transmission speeds than those provided by sending photocopies through the post.

Prophecies of libraries where the codex and the printed page have been replaced by digital storage devices and where a computing facility has taken over the task of literature searching is very exciting and attractive, both to librarians and to those scholars who really are overwhelmed by their century's information explosion. Although many people would regret the passing of the codex and although the combination of the printed page, the codex, and the library is embarrassingly efficient as a machine for storing data and providing rapid random access to it, there is no doubt that many research workers would welcome real assistance with their information gathering problems. Good assistance would be provided by a skilled librarian, but in a world where skilled people are in short supply it is likely that some machine system will eventually take over this task. The techniques that such a machine would use may be quite different from those now used in libraries, but the end result would be the same.

Our task as librarians is both to design these techniques and to see that we do not hinder their adoption, where appropriate, by arguing from emotion. One such technique, now with us, may be that of bibliographic coupling, and certainly the methods now being developed for machine processing of natural language texts will have an important role to play in the operation of this future automated library. Pattern of automated library service in the future can only be predicted by educated extrapolation of the developments that are taking place in libraries today, bearing in mind other factors which will have an important bearing on libraries.

Included among these will be an expected continuing exponential growth in population and the increasing the importance of libraries in the developing countries.

The expansion of knowledge shows no signs of abating, and libraries will also be faced with a continuing proliferation of disciplines, coupled with a trend towards interdisciplinary study. The volume of publications will continue to grow but there should be an increasing recognition by central governments of the importance of libraries and their functions of bibliographic control and information dissemination. The consequence of this recognition will be greater financial support for library programmes. The key requirement in such an age is that libraries should be flexible. This will be manifested in all facets of librarianship; library buildings, systems for subject representation, forms of publications and the reader services provided for the library's clientele.

Co-operation between libraries at local, national, and international levels will increase in importance, but it must be flexible so as to ensure that individual, importance, but it must be flexible so as to ensure that individual, seemingly more important goals. Most important of all, perhaps, is the recognition that libraries serve as an intermediary in process of communication between human beings. They are not ends in themselves and the fact that libraries must deal ultimately with people, not merely with inanimate documents and machines, obliges us to design systems which treat both readers and library staff with understanding and respect for their personal feelings and needs.

The computer has a central role to play in such future library systems. As a reliable, competent, accurate, and cheap manipulator or library information it can bring to fruition many idealistic concepts about flexible library services. In that it has the capacity to free human beings from much of the repetitive labour that is a necessary concomitant to library work, it can also give us the opportunity to provide personal service to real people.

The necessary prerequisite to the wise and proper use of computing machinery in libraries in the future is a body of wise and informed library managers now. It is possible to distinguish two general directions in which computer aided services will develop. Printed lists prepared by computer processing of a basic corpus of bibliographic records will increase in number and in diversity, and facilities for on-lie interrogation of files held in machine memories will become more widely available. Computer-aided library systems almost invariably produce as their end product some sort of printed list for human consultation or scanning. We can expect to see more such lists prepared in circumstances where they can be justified either by reducing costs or increasing services.

At present, too, a number of experimental on-line library projects are either operational or under development. It is reasonable to suppose that these will be successful and will eventually find application in certain circumstances. It is possible to divide present-day on-line projects into two broad categories; those involving the automation of one or more library housekeeping functions, and those concerned with information retrieval and the processing of natural language text.The major area of library housekeeping which librarians tend to regard as being suitable for on-line methods is circulation control.

Although no system is operational yet, work is either in progress or under consideration at the University of California, San Diego and Los Angeles, and at Harwell and Belfast. A proposal for on-line accessing of periodicals has come from the University of Lancaster, and a number of libraries are considering systems for on-line manipulation and cataloguing data. Assuming that it remains essential to make non-programmable alterations either to ordering data or catalogue data from a central agency before it can be added to a library's own catalogue file, then an on-line visual display console equipped with a keyboard and light pen would appear to be an attractive piece of hardware for doing this. All of these on-line systems, however, involve only minor modifications to existing patterns of library activity.

More far-reaching changes to present-day methods of library use appear to be implied in on-line systems for information retrieval and text processing. Those that come closest to everyday library operations involve the on-line interrogation of a file of bibliographic records. This enables a search to be directed in the first place to the names of authors, editors, etc, titles, class numbers, or codex. Secondary search of a body of records retrieved by one of the above terms can be by means of a subject term; publisher's name, date of publication, place of publication, language, or location. The details of the system have yet to be worked out, including the bibliographic record format to be used, but the body of records will be indexed in four ways corresponding to the four data categories by which primary access to the file may be obtained.

Presumably, search statements can combine more than one term in logical relationship. A project is also under way to create an on-line union-catalogue for the public libraries of metropolitan Toronto. Here, in addition to the design of the machine system, difficulties have to be overcome in respect of the machine system, difficulties have to be overcome in respect of differences of cataloguing practice between co-operating libraries. It is likely that this project will provide for only limited degrees of search complexity, and will handle only abbreviated bibliographic records in order to minimise the size of file required. Kessler is conducting an interesting experimental project at Massachusetts Institute of Technology which permits on-line searching of bibliographical records by various novel search strategies.

Articles from twenty-one specially chosen physics journals are "indexed" for the system, but conventional subject indexing is not employed except in so far as it is made available in Physics Abstracts. Search strategies can be defined on the basis of journal titles, author's names and—words in titles. Citation-orientated searching is also possible, for example, one can search for all papers which cite a chosen article or alternatively, all papers that have a stated number of references in common with the chosen article. Kessler has introduced the concept of bibliographic coupling to describe the linkage formed between papers which have references in common.

Two papers are said to be bibliographically coupled with coupling strength of one (two, three etc.) when they have one (two, three etc.) references in common. Kessler has found that groups of papers coupled in this way are quite similar to the groups of papers coupled in this way are quite similar to the groups made by a conventional subject index. Indexing by means of bibliographic coupling is likely to become more common in future than it has been in the past. Relying on the authors of papers for the intellectual efforts which is required for a good index, it demands the use of new search strategies on the part of library users. The technique is particularly suitable for machine applications in that no intellectual effort is required to construct the index. The printed volumes of Science Citation Index are compiled on these principles and make it possible to experiment now with search strategies which will be appropriate with some future on-line information retrieval systems.

A detailed description of an imaginary on-line library system has been given by Licklider. Termed a "procognitive system" in that it exists for, or to serve, knowledge and learning, it replaces the codex and the card index of present-day libraries by direct-access computer memories containing the same information. Computer processors in the procognitive system are able, in an unspecified way, to organise and mull over the data in store, and also to search it.

A program named SYMBIONT enables a number of basic operations to be performed on textual matter. Once a document has been input to the system, 150-word "pages" of it can be displayed on the face of a console. Pages can be turned forwards and backwards, and selected passages of text can be named and stored for future reference. Searches can then be made using these names.

Project INTREX is another experiment in the same general direction. Begun in late 1965 it is a research programme whose main aim is to provide, a solution to the problems of large libraries by means of on-line computing techniques similar to those of SYMBIONT and the procognitive system. Automation being carried out by libraries is usually in acquisition, serials control, cataloguing, circulation and management statistics. Some progress has been made by the libraries in these areas.

A few institutions are cresting and maintaining bibliographic databases in machine readable form and bringing out lists, catalogues, union catalogues, etc. They offer current awareness service. Private software firms have recently started to develop library application software packages and they are made available on a commercial basis.

Some libraries and information centres have developed softwares in-house for specific application, with local expertise. Serious attention is now being paid to training aspect for developing skills in computer application among the library and information manpower. Computer application in library and information field has made phenomenal progress in industrialised countries where hardware, software and communications facilities are well developed. In view of their technological advancement, they are able to computerise their entire library and information system in the country, with great success.

Besides improving services and operations for a better performance, libraries are able to evolve effective computer networks, towards optimum utilisation of resources and facilities. International programmes like UNISIST/UNESCO, Universal Availability of Publications (UAP) and Universal Access to Information (UAI) and a few others have helped in promotion and coordination of information services through out the world.

Global information systems, characterised by decentralised input, centralised processing and decentralised distribution, such as INIS, AGRIS, and DEVSIS have been evolved towards universal bibliographic control and dissemination of literature. Major producers of secondary information services have become international information/database centres for their respective subjects/disciplines. Communication networks like TYMNET, TELENET and ESANET offer communication facilities to international information centres that offer database services. Towards promoting cooperative endeavours, regional networks like ASTINFO, RINSCA and TECHNONET and specialised networks like AIBA, INNERTAP, SEAMIC and others have come about. These are all useful international efforts in transborder flow of information and in diffusion of knowledge through out the word. The library networks in USA are in a most advanced level of development.

The favourable factors responsible for successful development of library networking in USA are long tradition of cooperation among libraries, introduction of library automation as early as from 1960's, advances in information science during 1970's and 1980's and introduction of MARC format by the Library of Congress in 1968.

The experiences of USA in library networking are valuable to our efforts in designing the INFLIBNET. Three foremost bibliographic utilities and networks in USA are the Online Computer Library Centre, Dublin, Ohio (OCLC), Research Libraries and Information Network, Stanford, California (RLIN) and Washington Library Network, Olympia, Washington (WLN). Library networking is based on three major areas of technology, viz., creation of bibliographic information in machine readable format for storage and retrieval, hardware/software for database use and services and telecommunication mechanism for transmission of information.

The major point of success of library network depends upon availability of machine readable catalogues in the constituent units. The latest trend is to use CD-ROM technology for storing the catalogue data. The OCLC, established in 1967, and has a staff of 812 persons is a non-profit organisation and supports resource sharing among more than 6,700 libraries in USA, besides countries in Europe, Saudi Arabia and Australia. Its union catalogue database contains 13 million records; some 30,000 records are added every week. With the steady growth of OCLC, there has been a progressive decline in the amount of original cataloguing to be done by the participating libraries. The system hit rate has increased from 66 per cent in 1971 to 94 per cent in 1983. The details about telecomn unication system, input sources. RLIN, established in 1978 and which has as staff of 81 persons, supports the cooperative programmes of Research Libraries Group, comprising 36 major libraries and other research institutions. It maintains 6 databases online.

The catalogue database holds more than 20 million records. WLN, established in 1972 and which has a staff of 51 persons, provides, more than 250 libraries in seven states of USA, online computerised services to promote resource sharing and automated library functions. The bibliographic file contains more than 3.5 million catalogue records.Information network is a set of interrelated information systems associated with communication facilities, which are cooperating through more or less formal agreements and institutional agreements, in order to jointly implement information handling operation, with a view to pooling their resources and to offer better services to the user. They generally follow identical or compatible rules and procedures.

A library network consists of six major components:

1) Information resources,
2) Reader or users of information,
3) Schemes for intellectual organisation of data/ documents,
4) Methods for the delivery of information to user- the output,

5) Formal organisation—cooperation, whether voluntary or obligatory, in information exchange and utilisation,

6) Bidirectional communication links.

There is also an enthusiasm among the professionals to get trained in library automation. As on date, nearly 50 library and information centres are known to be computerising their activities. There are possibilities of mounting bibliographical databases on these networks for providing online access to users. The University Library in Newcastle-upon-Tyne has been operating a computer-aided ordering system. The introduction of this system was facilitated in that it makes use of a number of programs already in existence as part of the Newcastle file-handling system. This is a suite of programs written for the English Electric KDF9 computer to facilitate the handling of structured data of the kind found in bibliographical applications.

It is interesting to note that Newcastle University library report a small saving in staff time compared with the previous order system which used edge-notched cards. If computer time were charged to the library, however, the automated system would be considerably more expensive.

For new books which are included in the Virginia Kirkus Service pre-punched cards are distributed, one for each title, giving the usual bibliographical information. To order one of these books all that a library has to do is to return the appropriate punched card to the data-processing centre indicating the number of copies needed. The University of Maryland operating an acquisitions system utilising punched-card equipment only. Orders and auxiliary listings of outstanding orders, receipts, and fund reports are made using an IBM 407 accounting machine. "On order" cards are filed manually in the public card catalogue and pre-cataloguing is carried out whenever complete Library of Congress cataloguing data is available.

Accounting costs are reduced to one thirteenth of their previous level by this very simple system which just uses the computer as a calculating machine. In libraries where funds are limited it is important to remember that modest automation programmers can result in significant savings which can be directed to improving conventional services. A unique computer-aided system for ordering replacement copies of standard books is now operating in Toronto. Public librarians there have selected a standard list of about 2500 titles, all of which are available in paperback editions.

Given information on the quality rating of publishers' editions, the computer prepares monthly lists of replacement orders which enable each branch library to have in stock a determined number of copies of all the standard titles, all in good condition. A number of library systems in the Toronto area are cooperating in this scheme which, because of its size enables substantial discounts to be obtained. A number of other libraries have reported automated acquisitions systems to be in operation. At the library of the University of Michigan a disc memory store is used in the computer processing of order records, while at the Redstone Scientific Information Center a system christened ALPHA (Automatic Literature, Processing, Handling, and Analysis) utilises an IBM 632 electronic typing calculator for key punching the original order records.University of Southampton operating a typical computer-aided circulation control system. It is being implemented in four stages of increasing sophistication the first of which commenced in operation.

The first stage, as a by-product of its operation, produces a book card for each book that is circulated, thus building up an active collection of books with books cards ready for automatic input of charging data during the second stage of the system. The final two stages provide for on-line interrogation and updating of the loans file. Borrowers fill in slips for each book they borrow and reserve and data-processing staff keypunch one card for each of these transactions and also one card for each book that is returned.

Advantage of a crash programme is that the circulation system can employ automatic collection of charging data right from the very beginning, and that there will be no need to cater for books being circulated without cards. Although cards will be made for many books which will in fact never be circulated again, it will not be necessary to punch cards for books that are returned as at Southampton.

Trueswell has shown that for a university technical library where it is the newest books that circulate most, it is more economical to prepare book cards for books on loan during the loan period than to carry out a crash programme for the entire collection. And if all new acquisitions are supplied with book cards at the technical processing stage, possibly as a by-product of an automated order system, then in time only a small percentage of books will be presented for circulation without book cards.

A number of libraries in the United States have now adopted circulation control systems based on either the IBM 357 or 1030 data-collection units, accepting data from eighty-column punched book cards and readers' plastic badge cards. Among these are Southern Illinois University, Florida Atlantic University, Lehigh University, Oak Ridge National

Laboratory, and the University of Missouri. An unusual system operates at Johns Hopkins University which represents one solution to the slow charging speeds which are associated with computer-aided circulation control. The price paid is an extra operation in the circulation procedure.

Charge and discharge data is captured on microfilm by photographing the reader's identification card and the spines of up to twelve or fifteen books being borrowed. After developing the film the data is keypunched and processed by the computer in the normal way. Two university libraries in Germany, Bochum and the Technical University of Berlin, have implemented automated circulation control systems using book cards edge-punched with paper-tape codes for automatic collection of charging data.

Circulation control systems using punched-card machines have not yet been displaced by computer-based systems. One has recently been installed in the Atomic Weapons Research Establishment at Aldermaston. It makes use of the card duplicating facility of an IBM 026 printing card punch to create three transaction cards for each loan from punched book and reader cards.

One card is filed manually in the issues file and the other two are used by a computer to apply various controls to the system; to test for overdue books, for example. Eighty-column cards are filled in by borrowers and then keypunched for processing. A computer is used only for printing letters recalling overdue books. Judging from the experience of the University of Hawaii it would be foolish to assume that computer-based circulation systems are the only ones worth introducing in this modern age. Libraries have produced lists of their periodicals holdings by computer punched-card methods and taken advantage of the opportunities thus afforded for distributing the list widely and updating it easily and frequently. A union list of periodicals held in Institute of Education libraries in Britain was also published in 1966. It was produced with the aid of some programs of the Newcastle file handling system.

Experiments are in hand to print new editions of this union list by computer typesetting techniques being developed by the University of Newcastle-upon-Tyne computer typesetting project. The main library at Harwell is responsible for purchasing periodicals for its own collections as well as for those of twenty-two divisional libraries.

The use of mechanised methods for compiling the list made it a comparatively simple job to supply each library within the system with a frequently updated union list of periodicals. The most important British union list of serials produced by mechanical means is, of course, the new BUCOP. Input is from punched cards and processing is done by IBM 1401 computer. In the case of a widely used list such as this it becomes important that computer typesetting techniques should be introduced quickly, even though the present frequently updated list is an immense improvement on the older ones. In Britain a computer-produced checking-in list has been developed at the City University.

Periodical parts expected to arrive during the coming month are listed on a line printer. As the parts are received in the library they are ticked off on this list, making it a simple matter to inform library users about the arrival or non-arrival of a particular journal issue. This printed checking-in list gives full titles of journals, unlike systems which punch an eighty-column card for each expected part, where title have to be abbreviated. The system is capable of conversion to a fully automated one, which would require only a minimum amount of keypunching to cater for parts which do not behave as expected. Another semi-automated system has been installed at the Louisville School of Medicine, Louisville, Kentucky. Using only punched-card equipment, check-in cards are prepared for each expected title. These require the manual addition of volume number, part number, and date of receipt to complete the full bibliographical data for each part. The very simplest level at which entries for bibliographies and catalogues can be prepared by automated methods is that involving the use of a paper-tape typewriter or the IBM Document Writer. These machines are used widely in libraries nowadays and their routine application is seldom reported in the literature.

Two useful articles which explain how they have been used in particular libraries are those by Wilson and Bernstein. Conflicting reports have been published on the relative costs of producing catalogue cards by tape typewriter and by other techniques. Mackenzie shows the tape typewriter to be about 75 per cent as costly as either a stencil duplicator or a small offset litho machine. Moore, on the other hand, finds the reverse to be true-duplicating methods works out to be approximately 75 per cent as costly as tape typewriters.

The cause of these divergent results is to be found in the relative amounts of clerical time stated to be required by the two methods. An interesting variation on these methods has been reported by Fasana et al. Catalogue records are prepared in machine-readable form and in a special machine-interpretable natural format using a tape typewriter. Working from the tape punched by the tape typewriter, a special digital machine-the Itek Crossfiler-prepares a catalogue entries.

Running this second tape through a tape typewriter produces the required card set directly. Briefly, this technique obviates the need to use a program tape when added entries are being typed and makes for greater flexibility in the production of added entries of different kinds. There is a large literature dealing with various aspects of the production of card and book catalogues by means of punched cards and computer methods.

Dewey gives a brief historical survey of the earliest catalogues produced by punched-card methods and records that the first non experimental catalogue of books was made in 1951 for the branch libraries of King County (Washington) Public Library System. More widely known are the book catalogues of Los Angeles Country Public Library, first introduced in 1953. Before that date only 26 of the system's 114 service outlets had card catalogues, while the introduction of book catalogue enabled each branch to have a union catalogue of the whole library system.

A book catalogue produced by punched-card methods was introduced to the science and engineering libraries of the University of Rochester in 1962. This short-title catalogue, now made using an IBM 7094 computer, is designed as a supplement to the libraries' regular card catalogues and each entry is accordingly limited to one line only. In the latest editions of this catalogue refinements have been made to the sort programs. Among the North American libraries that have made book catalogues by computer are Stanford University Library, where the decision to automate was based on a thorough comparative cost analysis, Florida Atlantic University, where the original intention was that the catalogue should also be searchable by machine and Toronto University Library, which prepared a book catalogue of the combined holdings of five new university libraries in the province of Ontario—the ONULP project. At Harvard University Library a project is under way to convert the entire shelf list to machine-readable form.

In that a shelf list is a classified sequence of bibliographic records, the whole job can conveniently be split into small units and one main class keypunched at a time. The first Harvard class, the Crusades, was completed in May 1965. As with the short title catalogue at the University of Rochester, these printed shelf lists, invaluable as they are, can only be regarded as supplements to the main card catalogue where full bibliographic details are available.Each class of the Library of Congress shelf list would be converted and machine printout compared with the holdings of other large research libraries. They would add to the machineable records their own locational symbols and titles held only by them, and could print their own book catalogues by selective listing of the master tapes.

The medical libraries of Yale University and Columbia University are co-operating in a project which will eventually provide them with a common pool of books and journals the catalogue of which will be in machineable form and accessible through remote on-line consoles. An unusual computer-produced catalogue on microfilm has been operational in the Technical Information Center of Lockheed Missiles and Space Company since July 1966.

Using a machine to compose directly from the computer onto microfilm is stated to reduce costs considerably. Access to the catalogue must be by means of a microfilm reader, but film kept in cartridge makes for simple handling and a Xerox Copyflo can be used to produce hard copy quickly and cheaply if this is wanted. The Library of Congress project MARC has had a marked influence on libraries' plans for catalogue automation both in North America and Britain. The MARC pilot project, in which cataloguing copy was distributed on an experimental basis to sixteen libraries, began in October 1966 and is still continuing. At the time of writing, the Library of Congress is developing an improved format for the catalogue records on MARC tapes, designed to facilitate the communication of bibliographic data in machineable form.

Coward describes this new format and discusses the United Kingdom MARC service, which is hoped to be made available within the next few years. It will be firmly based on co-operation with the next few years. It will be firmly based on co-operation has already been established in regard to the actual data going into catalogue records as part of the Library of Congress Shared Cataloguing Program. Introduction of standard book numbering to the British book trade has provided a convenient tag for identifying the records on the British MARC tapes and should reduce greatly the problems associated with matching catalogue records by computer.

A possible file structure for the weekly magnetic tapes produced by the U.K. MARC service might be as follows: firstly, a main file consisting of a series of catalogue records in standard book number order; and secondly, a title index to the first part of the file. The index might also be produced in printed form along with a listing of the SBN's of records in the first part of the file.

The public library systems of the London Boroughs of Barnet, Camden, and Greenwich have had computer-produced book catalogues for nearly 3 years now. Using the services of a computer bureau and accepting severe limitations on the format and layout of entries, these libraries have been able, nevertheless, to improve their public services by supplying all branches with union catalogues, a virtual impossibility with a manual system. At the Cambridge Philosophical Library project has commenced to produce by computer a union catalogue of books in the many departmental libraries with in the University of Cambridge.

The entire shelf lists of a sample of these libraries are being converted into machineable form and a thorough investigation will be made into the problems of merging the separate catalogues at the University of Rochester. Unless entries referring to identical books really are truly identical the computer will include them both in the updated catalogue. In Germany, book-form catalogues are being produced by computer at the University of Bochum. This is a new university and in fact has no card catalogue at all. Germany has also made an important contribution to computer-aided cataloguing methods by being the first country to produce its national bibliography by computer.

The effect of automation are the following:

1. Extent of cataloguing information presented to the users
2. Choice of information given
3. Arrangement of information
4. Typographical presentation of such information.

Librarians have bemoaned the upper case mentality of computers and related machines since their use in library work began. The resulting catalogues were certainly less attractive and less readable than the printed or typed cards with which most people were familiar. Within a few months of Clapp's talk, however, the situation began to change. It did cost a substantial amount in computer processing time.

however, which led to its abandonment by Atlantic University. Photocomposition machines, which did not share this handicap, later became available, and in some cases offered the additional advantage of a wider variety of type faces and images than older printing techniques.

Microform catalogues and computer terminal displays have encountered the same problem, but both have now advanced at least to the stage that acceptable upper and lower case characters in the Roman alphabet are available. Non-Roman alphabets and nonalphabetic characters are still a problem, but the capacity for providing these exists if the demand becomes sufficient. Changes in the extent of cataloguing information presented to the user under each entry have been mainly deletions rather than additions, and such changes are most frequently seen in book catalogue projects. Virtually every descriptive element has been eliminated or abbreviated in one project or another.

The Boeing SLIP catalogue restricts author's fore-names to one and represents the others by initials; other catalogues give only initials, with no fore-names. The University of Rochester catalogues limit the main entry to twenty-one spaces, with necessitates a substantial amount of abbreviation in corporate authors. Collation is perhaps the most frequently abridged set of elements. Standford and Florida Atlantic give pagination only, and many catalogues give no collation at all.

Notes and tracings are also frequently omitted, with the exception of series and contents notes in a few cases. The ONULP (Ontario New University Libraries Project) catalogues, however give full tracings under main entries, as does the National Library of Medicine Current Catalogue, the latter because other medical libraries use the catalogue as a source of cataloguing information. In many catalogues the amount and type of abridgement varies according to the type of entry involved. Normally the main entry is reasonably full, and most abbreviation or abridgement takes place in added entries.

In the Los Angeles County catalogue, however, the subject entries are more complete than the author entries, because the subject entries include an annotation. The practice of abridging entries has been justified on several grounds. Undoubtedly it began, especially in catalogues produced with unit record equipment such as the University of Rochester listings, because of the eight-column limitation of punched cards and the printing limitations of tabulators.

As Weinstein and George have noted, the one-to-one, punched card/printed line relationship, and line-length/field-length compromises, all encourage brevity of entry. At least in part, however, the elimination of data elements also reflect a desire to cut costs. Simonton has viewed it as a reflection of the traditional policy of many of these libraries of shortening the bibliographical record for more economical processing.

Another justification is based on the shorter life expectancy of the book catalogue as compared to the traditional card catalogue:

> As [card] catalogues serve as the basis for the permanent record and their cost can be prorated over several decades the need for a careful description of the many facets of a book is quite properly justified. In the case of a book is quite properly justified. In the case of catalogue supplements, however, where the record will serve quite likely for only a few

> months, any attempt at detailed description of the book cannot be justified.

As might perhaps be expected, the old argument over whether the catalogue serves as a bibliographical tool or a finding list has also been revised. Robinson, for example, writes about the planing for the Baltimore Country book catalogue project:

> We also agreed on the concept that this catalogue was to be a finding list, not a bibliographical tool. We had always done fairly simplified cataloguing anyway, and frankly, we were convinced that, as bibliographical tools, catalogue are vastly overrated and underused anyway. Taking an educated guess, we estimated that only 50 percent of the people who come into out libraries use the catalogue at all, and 98 percent of those use it as a finding list.

Not all changes in the extent of cataloguing information presented have been abridgements or deletions, however; some writers and projects, in fact, have seen automation as a means of increasing the amount of information made available. Many catalogues of special libraries have provided additional subject headings, however, taking advantage of the ease with which machines can reproduce entries under various headings.

Most book catalogues also reproduce title entries for all items in the catalogue, not just those with distinctive titles, and as mentioned in the discussion of the Boeing SLIP catalogue some also permute the titles so that they appear several times for each work, under each significant word in each title. The choice of main entry has long been a critical issue in cataloguing policy and in the development of cataloguing rules, but with the advent of machine-produced book catalogues the need for the concept of "main entry" may be questioned. When catalogue cards were printed or typed by hand, it made economic sense to produce only one card, with the data arranged in a standard format under a "main entry," and then to reproduce other cards as needed, typing only the added headings required after the "unit cards" had been duplicated.

Computers, however, can rearrange data in any fashion deemed appropriate, so this rationale is no longer applicable. Despite this fact, many book catalogue continue to follow the unit card and main entry concepts. The ONULP catalogues. For example, print the author under each title entry, and then repeat the title a practice that would appear to have no justification except for mechanically reproduced catalogue cards. A few book, catalogue projects have abandoned this anachronistic practice and reproduce entries under various headings without any attempt to designate one as the main entry, even though the entries under each heading are still unit entries.

Abandonment of the main entry concept, it should be pointed out, also means abandoning and attempt to designate the person or body primarily responsible for the intellectual content of a work, but clearly it makes the choice of entry less critical, particularly in difficult case such as conference proceedings, where the choice between conference title, sponsoring body or editor may be little more than arbitrary. One of the greatest effects of automation on cataloguing practice to data has been in the arrangement of entries in relation to each other.

Virtually all book catalogues are divided catalogues, abandoning the so-called dictionary arrangement that interfiles all types of entries in a single sequence. The type of division is not consistent from one catalogue to another. Some have separate author, title, and subject sections; some combine author and title entries in one catalogue with a separate subject section; and at least one combines titles and subjects, with the author entries separate.

Regardless of the method of division, however, two principal reasons are usually given for the arrangement: users make different uses of subject entries as opposed to author and title entries, according to a number of user studies, and the filing or sequencing of entries can be simplified if all types of entries are not interfiled. The latter reason is normally the more urgent when automation is involved. Catalogues can be divided without being automated, and if ease of use were the only justification for division there would be no reason to attribute the popularity of the practice to automation. Filing, however, is another matter, and simplification of filing for automation purposes is undoubtedly the main reason for the predominance of the practice. Computers can sequence and arrange data with extreme speed and accuracy if given explicit rules for doing so, but traditional library filing arrangements are a mixture of alphabetical, chronological and other sequences presumed to be logical, with numerous general and specific exceptions. In addition to the complexity of the rules, many of them are based on the ability of human filers to recognize information that is only implicit, not explicitly stated, and computers can work only with explicit data. At least five categories of difficulty may be identified:

1) Information in the headings must be ignored or removed in order fore computers to sort it acceptably. Honorific titles such as "Sir" in proper names are also commonly disregarded, so that "Drake, Sir Francis" files as "Drake, Francis."

2) Information that is implicit must be made explicit. A common example is "U.S.—History—Civil War," which as a subdivision of "U.S.—History" files not alphabetically under "C" but chronologically, as if it were "U.S.—History—1861-1865." This category of problems is perhaps the most difficult for computers to deal with because there are no clues for most such instances, sand the number of "as if" situations in most current filing practices is large. It is also the least defensible. "Dr." is filed as if were spelled "Doctor" or "Doktor," depending on the language of the text, nut if the reader does not know the rule, or has only a title such as "Dr. Jacob Dubs" to go on, he may miss the entry entirely. "Mrs.," and presumably "Mac," although McKenzies insist they are not Mackenzies. Numbers are a special example of the "as if" problem; they file as if spelled out at the beginning of titles, but file as numbers, in numerical sequence, in headings for numbered conferences, series and so forth.

3) Information in headings must be rearranged in order for machines top sort it into the desired sequence. "Charles II, King of England" must be read as 'charles, King of England, II"—or actually, since there is also a numeral in this case and the second category of difficulty comes into play, as "Charles, King of England, 2."

4) Exceptions must be made to alphabetic order. Some rules require that entries beginning with the same word or phrase be sub-arranged not alphabetically by the next filing element but by bibliographic function (authors, then subjects, then titles, for example), or according to the type of entity the heading describes (persons), then places, then things).

5) Punctuation is even a problem, because of complications introduced both by the machines and by filing rules. Computers regard punctuation marks as character just as letters and numerals, and sort them into a certain order (differing to some extent by brand of machine) unless programmed to do otherwise. Extra spaces inadvertently inserted by humans will affect machine filing order as well. Existing rules differ on the treatment of certain marks, for example, whether "Brewer's Dictionary of Phrase and Fable" should be filed as "Brewers" or "Brewers," and "Mott-Smith" as "Mott Smith" or "MottSmith."

Ideal solution to these various problems is unclear, but attempts to solve them in automated catalogues have produced a significant amount of change as compared with manually filed catalogues. Most projects have used a combination of four basic approaches:

1) Continue to follow present filing rules, using people to assign additional codes to headings as necessary to allow computers to arrange the headings as desired.

2) Abandon present filing rules, and use the arrangements produced by the computer's sorting sequences with a minimum amount of change.

3) Change the headings themselves as necessary so that computers can arrange them in accordance with very simple filing rules.

4) Attempt to program computers so that they will arrange headings automatically, either by present filing rules or by modifications of them.

The first approach in its book catalogue, used nonfile symbols to indicate to the computer that portions of an entry were to be ignored in filing. Determination of when the symbols were to be added and actually adding them were of course operations performed by human beings. Use of the symbols was limited to initial articles, qualifying phrases such as "jt. author," and titles of honour; for example, "Churchill, Sir Winston," was input as "Churchill, Sir Winston," to enable it to sort as "Churchill, Winston." Umlauted letters were converted to letters without the umlaut, but followed by an "e." Unfortunately, this also meant that "cooperate" became "co-operate," and "Bronte" became "Brontee." Abbreviations were filed as written, not as if spelled out, and "Mc" was filed as "Mc." A more thoroughgoing example of the first approach is the Stanford Undergraduate Library book catalogue published first in 1966.

A considerable amount of manual coding was performed in the University's main card catalogue. Entries were sorted not on the text of the entries themselves but on separate "sort keys" composed of a total of 100 characters, 80 from the filing element and 20 additional characters from the title, which was used throughout the catalogue for subarrangement of entries under each heading. An obvious disadvantage of extended use of sorting and filing codes was noted at Stanford: the technique requires manual maintenance of authority files, very careful inputting, and very careful editing and proofreading.

The second alternative had attempted few projects because of the radical differences from traditional filing that would result, but a number of catalogues have used the third approach—changing the headings so the computer would arrange them in accordance with simplified but more or less traditional filing rules. Usually such projects have taken a strictly pragmatic approach, solving the simplest problems and ignoring the others. The Baltimore County book catalogue, first published in 1965, is an example. Initial articles, titles of honour and such designations as "ed." or "comp." were omitted from headings during input, which of course meant that they were ignored not only in filing but also in printing. Abbreviations, numerals, and symbols such as the ampersand were written out. Foremost advocates of changing headings to produce the desired sequence have been Theodore Hines and Jessica Harris.

In 1963, Hines urged that "filing should be a purely mechanical operation which can be reduced to a straight forward arrangement of sorts and nuls. The filer or program should not be expected to expand or interpret entries for filing purposes. These functions should be shifted to the formation of entries." Publication of the Hines-Harris code created a storm of protest. One reviewer warned, "This little book seems likely to do more harm than good. The end it proposes may be laudable, but the means are not. The book rests on the proposition that what is awkward for the machines must be eliminated and the simplicities of the machine system imposed on non-machine processes."

The fourth approach is the extreme—attempting to program the computer to follow traditional rules as closely as possible— was taken by William R. Nugent of Inforonics, Inc., in a study commissioned by the Council on Library. Resources. Unlike most proposals which advocated sorting abbreviations and similar exceptional cases "as is" rather than "as if," Nugent proposed a system of "substitution notes" which would continue traditional "as if" filing. Extensive rules to permit arrangements by category were also suggested. In not every case, however, was Nugent happy with his assignment to propose ways of programming the LC Filing Rules. If one set out deliberately to destroy the simple precision of numerical hierarchy, little worse could be done than to insist that numbers be ordered by the spelled out equivalents of their spoken sound.

In this writer's view, the present filing rule should be quickly replaced by one in which all cardinal or ordinal numbers, whether in alphabetic or numeric from, would be ordered by their elementary numeric from. As this is unlikely to occur with any haste, it will probably be necessary to write programs to covert the numeric portions of entries to alphabetic from. He then pointed out that it would be necessary to devise further rules to ensure consistency, because "1810" could be written out as "eighteen ten," "one thousand eight hundred ten" or "one eight one and the existing LC Rules convert such numbers "to differing forms by application of some unspecified and doubtless unprogrammable subtlety."

This kind of problem of necessity led Nugent to propose various types of manual coding as well as elaborate programming. In February 1970, John C. Rather, the then Chief of the Technical Process Research Office in the Library of Congress distributed a working paper entitled *Filing Arrangement in the Library of Congress Catalogs* within LC and to a limited extent outside it, setting forth a series of principles and basic approaches. Consensus within the Library led to public distribution of a full set of rules with the same title the following year. In 1972, the principles and basic approaches were elaborated in print, accompanied by an abridged version of the rules. They have since been used as the basis for a computer program to arrange MARC records and produce a variety of book catalogs for LC. Since they are also being considered for using in automatic preparation of the National Union Catalogue, their significance is obvious. Rather is eloquent on the dangers of changing headings merely because of the filing difficulties they present in automated systems. The complexities of catalogue headings and their arrangement are not attributable primarily to the rules that govern them; they arise from the varieties of materials being catalogued and the size of the catalogue being maintained. The need to differentiate names in the catalogue while still conveying intelligible information about the name result in forms of heading that indubitably present difficulties of arrangement. The fundamental conflict between the function of headings as units of intelligence and their function as filing guides cannot be underestimated, but the integrity of the heading must necessarily take precedence over any attempt to structure it so that it files "automatically." Or, to put the matter succinctly, headings do not exist merely to be filed. Rather thus eschews revision of headings for the sake of filing convenience, but he also advocates abandonment of the "as if" or "file as spoken" tradition, and for essentially the same reasons.

Variations in form among name and subject headings are an essential part of the structure of a file arrangement; they should not be ignored in filing. It is illogical to construct a heading on way and then to file it as if it were constructed another way. The three basic principles of his code are:

1) Elements in a heading should be taken in exactly the form and order in which they appear.

2) Related entries should be kept together if they would be difficult to find when a user did not know their precise from.

3) A standard set of fields should be established for each major type of filing entry.

The first principle emphasizes the way a heading looks, not how it sounds, the second preserves important values offered by the present arrangement of the LC catalogues, and the third applies the legal precept *De minimis non curat lex* (the law cannot take care of trifles) as a way of preventing the proliferation of special rules. Since Rather's rules have already met with general acceptance at LC and been used to produce several book catalogs, and since a computer program already exists to arrange MARC entries following these rules, their influence is likely to be evident in cataloguing practice for some time to come. The use of on-line techniques is another important influence on the arrangement of cataloguing information.

By 1968, Stanford University's on-line BALLOTS project had evolved a technique of filing machine-readable catalogue entries not by any of the usual rules, but in an arbitrarily arranged file with indexes by various bibliographic elements, such as author, title, topical subjects, and so forth. The significant and important aspect of the technique, however, was that the position of each entry in the author and title indexes was computed directly from the data itself, using the first three letters from the author's last name and the words of the title.

Availability of computer processing time has been a problem for numerous library projects; the lack of priority given by the computer centre to the development of library systems has been another complaint; and a third is the lack of control by the library over decisions regarding continuation of a project. A fourth problem involving computer centres and their personnel is what Veaner has called "system instability".

In a survey of twenty-four institutions conducted in 1972, he fond that this was more the rule than the exception, especially in software, operating systems, hardware configuration, and pricing. Wherever an academic computer facility was used for library development, the same broken record always seemed to be playing: the facility was always being taken apart and put together again. Ignorance of libraries and their operations has frequently led to a assumption that the problems to be solved are simple or trivial, or at best, to the glib conclusion by systems analysts and programmers that they understand both the problems and the solutions, Elitism—"the notion that the masters of the computer are inherently superior to and have better judgment than computer customers"—is also common. A relate problem is the fact that most of the good programmers and systems analysts are naturally interested in facing new challenges and are apt to become disinterest in library projects once they become "production" systems.

And ear also may play a part; to many computer centres, it has sometimes appeared that the library, in addition to its usually well-established role on campus or in the community, could become the largest of the computer centre's users, and in some facilities this recognition may have induced a fear of being taken over or overwhelmed by the user, who would then be in a position to dominate and dictate the direction of further development an operations.

Five type of problems can be identified on this category. The first is the failure of suppliers to deliver the necessary equipment. The Orange Country Public Library designed and programmed a circulation system but never implement it, simply because the company which was supposed to supply the hardware never delivered. A more common problem is the failure of suppliers to deliver the required software, either on time or at all. A third familiar problem is inadequate service, which plagued most of the projects using paper-tape machines and still troubles most libraries using automation projects are simply poor machines, either poorly engineered or poorly built, a case in point being the IBM 1050 which most libraries have discontinued using because of constant breakdowns.

The most serious problem originating with the library staff itself is the failure to distinguish legitimate research and experimentation from operational improvements, or to provide separate funds for research. Some of the development in library automation have been funded by grants but most have been funded from the operating budgets of individual libraries.

Only a few libraries have deliberately set aside a portion of their budgets for research ad experimentation. Because most experimental techniques were attempted under the guise of operational improvements, those that did not work were considered failures by the librarians. Money that have been used for more books or more staff had been wasted, it appeared, and mismanagement or misjudgment was often suggested.

Yet see properly as needed research and experimentation—the only way a profession advances—many of these failures were in fact successes. To the extent that they demonstrate methods which did not work, they made a valuable contribution to this part of librarianship. The real failure of many librarians involved in these projects is the lack of reporting to the profession on the problems encountered.

A few projects have been reported frankly and in full, but most have die silently, almost secretly. Perhaps because they were intended to be immediate operating improvements, their cessation was viewed with embarrassment and even shame, and those in charge refused to discuss them. In such cases, the failure goes beyond the mere missing of an opportunity to contribute to the advancement of the profession; a real harm results, because other libraries are apt to repeat the process with the same results, needlessly wasting money, manpower, and time. Networks have had a particularly high mortality rate, especially those designed to do centralized processing, but reports by the librarians involved on the reasons for discontinuance tend to be elusive. The Association of New York Libraries for Technical Services (ANYLTS) began like Florida Atlantic University with a considerable amount of publicity, and some $2.5 million was reported spent on its development, yet when it died in 1972 there was no general report to the profession.

Apparently development efforts had fallen considerably behind schedule, and the income-producing activities of the project could not sustain it after Federal funds were with drawn. In the absence of a formal report, however, it is impossible to know for certain the reasons for its failure.

Despite the stability of long-established procedures, another problem in many library automation projects has been that the library staff really did not understand the existing procedures, at least not with the precision and detail required for designing alternative methods of accomplishing the same tasks. As a result, systems were implemented which could not handle various exceptions to normal procedures, simply because the exceptions were not maintained or understood, and not uncommonly the whole project failed as a result.

Library staff have also created problems by failing to agree on the desired characteristics of the final product of a system. As might be imagine, cooperative projects and networks have been particularly vulnerable to this vice. The Colorado Academic Library

Book Processing Center (CALBPC) died in part because the participants constantly disagreed on the format of the catalogue cards all of them were to receive, some cataloguers insisting on treating cards as works of art, others insisting on petty variations to suit local conditions, and still others insisting on the maximum in economy.

The CALBPC effort also exposed other difficulties librarians seem to have in working with each other, such as head librarians feuding or jockeying for status, institutional jealousies, and simple parochialism.Problem that have troubled library automation projects are not the sole province of any one of the above group of people, but may originate with any or all of them. The first category of such problem may be thought of generally as poor planning, and at the head of the list of planning problems may be idea to initiate a project in the first place.

There are many valid reasons to begin an automated systems, or to provide a new service provided of course that the resources are available to pay for it. But many projects have been started, not for any of these reasons but because of pressure from the institution's administration to "be modern" or "automate the library", to keep up with the responses of the library world, to promote a personal reputation, or simply because somebody on the library staff is gadget-happy and needs a new toy.

Systems thus initiated, or begun without sufficient analysis of the goals and objectives of the project, are apt to fail early, and even if they proceed past the implementation stage lack of clearly define objectives will awake evaluation of their success difficult if not impossible. Another problem in planning that is frequently encountered is the lack of market research—that is, the failure to establish in advance that the planned product or service is needed or wanted.

The reports of the Washington University School of Medicine library on its book catalogue and serials list project provide good examples of this problem, as well as a related one: the products cost too much for the benefits derived. These twin problems—insufficient demand and inordinate costs—run through the reports of many troubled projects and seem to be the principal reasons for the failure of every example of a particular type of network not yet mentioned: the kind set up to transmit materials between libraries by facsimile transmission instead of by conventional interlibrary loan techniques.

The best-documented and most extensive such project was the Facsimile Transmission System (FACTS) in New York State, which involved fifteen libraries and ran from January 20, 1967 to March 31, 1968. An impressive amount of time and money was spent in constructing this network, but the results in terms of user response were disappointing. Apparently the principal problem was that there was little demand for the fast but expensive service the system was set up to provide.

Perhaps the biggest problem at the planning stage is simply wishful thinking. Unrealistic assumption are commonly made regarding the time required to complete and implement a project, the effort involved, and most of all the cost. Assumptions regarding the benefits that will result may also be at fault, a problem experienced by the Colorado Academic Libraries Book Processing Center. It was presumed at the planning stage that larger discounts would result if book orders were pooled, but in fact this never happened.

Libraries were not buying the same titles as much as had been though, and even when they did, it was it different times so the orders could not be pooled. With the added costs of processing, bookkeeping, and paperwork at the Center, the cost was higher, in fact, than if each library had ordered its books separately.

In their early enthusiasm and eagerness to get started, library system planners may also forget to do their homework—that is, to search the literature, to learn (through various means, including contact with the professional associations) of similar projects which have been attempted or implemented, and then to take the experiences of these projects into account. For a profession with the communication of information as a goal, the incidence of this failure is disturbing. The numerous information retrieval projects of the previous decade were particularly guilty in this regard, but examples exist for virtually every type of project.

Even terminal-oriented circulation systems, of which hundreds now exist, continue to be developed from scratch, without building on the experience of others. In some cases, this failure to profit from the lessons learned and the work done by other systems occurs not because of ignorance but because of what Brong and Pasternak have called the "N-I-H" or "Not-invented-Here" syndrome. The planners know of other systems which do what they wish to do, but they refuse to adopt such systems (or even to study them) simply because they were developed by other institutions.

The excuse may be that the existing systems were designed for public institutions rather than private ones (or vice versa), or that they do not accommodate "local conditions," but the real reasons are often ambition, arrogance, and indifference.

Occasionally the planning for a system is based on the existence of "soft" money—i.e., money from grants or one-time gifts or appropriations—or the assumption that such money will be available to fund the project in the future.

This is both appropriate and desirable if the project is developmental or experimental and designed either to terminate when the funds run our or to continue operating with identified, regularly budgeted funds. Incredible as it may seem, however, not a few projects have either assumed that soft money would continue to be available indefinitely, or have simply failed to consider what would happen when such funds ran out.

Design of many systems also falls prey to wishful thinking and unwarranted assumptions. For example, that acquisition data can be reused, without major changes, for catalogue cards, or that serials are regular and predictable enough that irregular serials will not be a major problem.

System designs may also fail to provide for editing and proofing procedures, as in the Florida Atlantic book catalogue project, where it was assumed that untrained clerical personnel could be relied on to code Library of Congress copy for keypunching without having their work revised. And some systems have omitted routines for handling exceptional circumstance, which again may be due to wishful thinking. Another problem associated with the design stage is poor choice of hardware.

The machinery chosen may be satisfactory for the functions it was originally designed to perform, but unsuitable for use in another context. Equipment designed for intermittent use may fail when used in a high-volume, production environment; and conversely, equipment designed for constant use may fail when used intermittently, as was the case in the Hawaii facsimile system.

Occasionally the misuse of hardware or software occurs because the designer has a pet technique, or a pet piece of equipment, and attempts to apply it to every system problem, simply because it is familiar and has worked for him before. A good systems designer starts by analysing the problem, conceptualizing alternative approaches to a solution, rigorously determining the advantages and disadvantages of each approach, and selecting one. If the project is large, specifications will then be drawn up, and only then will equipment selection begin. Unfortunately poor designers sometimes reverse the process and a poor system is almost inevitable. Occasionally, too, a particular designer or approach becomes a favourite not of a particular person but of a large number of libraries; in short, a fad.

A common fault is that those charge with the implementation, whether librarians, systems people, or administrative staff, fail to take the human element and human values sufficiently into account. Unless it is made clear to all staff members affected by the new system that the goal is better service or more assistance by the purpose of the system are understood, fears for job security are likely to be rampant even if not expressed, and failure to provide reassurances on this score can have serious repercussions. Temporary inconveniences or additional workloads caused by the one-time necessity of converting records must be explained, and disruptions must be anticipate and counteracted. Presumably back-up procedures will have been incorporated in the system during the design phase, but manual back-up procedures must also be provided during implementation in the event of total system failure.

Throughout design and implementation, documentation of the system and all procedures must also be produced, and some library systems have come to grief on this matter alone. A system may be implemented and working well, but if knowledge of the system is partly or fully in some key person's head and that person leaves or his services are otherwise lost, the solution of subsequent problems may be difficult if not impossible.

All systems change, or a least should change, since any library is growing and the requirements imposed on the system consequently differ. If documentation is faulty, changing the system may be a major problem, even in some instances enough to cause its abandonment. Any catalogue of woe such as the foregoing is naturally depressing, and inevitably runs the risk of seeming overdrawn. Fortunately there have been many systems that avoid most if not all of the problems cited, and successes probably outnumber the failures. Library automation is basically healthy, despite the problems mentioned, but it will more so when all of these involved can discuss, openly and candidly, the difficulties and even the failures that all sooner or later experience. The recent history of library automation systems is characterized by several strong trends brought about by changes both in technology and in the economic situation confronting most libraries. Unless radical change in either technology or the economy occur, these trends seem likely to continue dominant, and to determine the course of library automation development for some time to come.

Networks come in many styles and flavours. One of the most common is the cooperative center for providing catalogue cards (and sometimes relate cataloguing products), of which the outstanding and most successful example is OCLC, the Ohio College

Center. As mentioned earlier, many other state and regional network are now tied into OCLC and dependent on it to a greater or lesser extent for the services they offer.

These include NELINET (the New England Library Information Network of about 40 libraries); FAUL (the Five Associate University Libraries of Upstate New York, which despite the name includes seven members, one of which is not a university libraries); SUNY (the State University of New York, with seventy-two libraries); the Pittsburgh Regional Library Center; PALINET (the Pennsylvania Area Library Network); SOLINET (the Southeastern Library Network, with almost 100 members); the Cooperative College Library Center in Atlanta, Georgia; and AMIGOS (which stands for nothing in particular, but includes several dozen libraries in Texas and the Southwest organized into a network by the Interuniversity Council).

Another type of network is also concerned primarily with technical processing, but attempts to provide a means of cooperative acquisitions as well as cataloguing. Successful ones (at least if success is measured by continued operation) include the BCL (Books for College Libraries) program in Massachusetts and the College Bibliocentre program in Ontario, Canada. The mortality rate for this kind of network is high, however, as the deaths of CALBPC (the Colorado Academic Library Book Processing Center) and ANYLTS (the Association of New York Libraries for Technical Services) make clear.

A third type of grouping sometimes called a network is merely a loose consortium of libraries with special procedures for expediting interlibrary loans, often using teletypes. Most of these are not automated in any significant way, and so lie outside the sphere of this book, but some have been working for years to implement on-line networks for the same purposes, a prime example being NYSILL, the New York State Interlibrary Loan Network.

Most of networks would have to be labelled "in planning" or "in process of implementation", which some efforts dating back several years. CAPTAIN (Computer Aided Processing & Terminal Access Information Network) is intended to handle acquisitions and processing for New Jersey's eight state collages, but despite occasional signs of life has experienced constant difficulties in becoming fully operational. MALCAP (the Mary land Academic Library Center for Automated Processing) has had a similar experience. The universal interest in networks has several causes for one thing, declining library budgets and the startling increase in book and serial costs have made the need for cooperation between libraries more urgent. "Resource-sharing" has become a byword, and the resources implied are both bibliographical and financial.

On-line networks enable libraries to know quickly and efficiently which books are in other libraries, and it thus among a group of libraries, reducing the number of duplicate copies needed. Bibliographical data can be shared more effectively, too as the OCLC system demonstrates. The sources of funds for purely local automation projects have almost dried up; the Federal grants that were plentiful in the 1960s disappeared in the 1970s, foundations have been less willing to fund projects unless they were truly innovative, and most libraries own budgets are being held static or reduced instead of being increased. Money for cooperative projects that can reasonably be expected to reduce operating costs can usually be found, but not money for local experimentation.The improvement in communication between computer systems and system users has already been noted, but it should be pointed out that this extends to communication between libraries as well. Telephones and teletype have long made some interlibrary communication possible, but on-line networks allow librarians in many different libraries literally to share the same working files and catalogues in real time, almost as if they were working in one giant library.

Technology has also lowered the cost of storing units of data by several orders of magnitude and the cost of on-line terminals has declined almost as dramatically, while labour costs have continued to rise. Work in the development of standards has also facilitated networking. Without MARC as a national standard for machine-readable bibliographic data, most of the successful networks would not have been possible, and credit for this success must go not only to MARC's brilliant developers at the Library off Congress but also to the many librarians and others who worked hard to promote widespread acceptance of the standard though professional organizations such as the American Library Association, especially its Information Science and Automation Division Standards Institute and the International Standards Organization.

The recent introduction of International Standard Bibliographic Descriptions for monographs and serials opens the way for standard Serial Number offers promise for eventual control of what sticky body of data. The problems many libraries have experienced in using large, general-purpose institutional computers may also help account or the network trend, since a cooperative system used only for library purposes is one way of avoiding the necessity of sharing a computer with non-library users in an institutional environment. Another way around this problem, apart from networking, is the use of minicomputers owned, controlled and used solely by a single library, and this alternative appears to be growing in popularity. Mention has already been made of the library-owned 1440 used by the University of Missouri, and 1401s have also been dedicated to library purposes, notably at Harvard, and 1401s have also been dedicated to library purposes, notably at Harvard.

Minicomputers as currently defined are smaller than the 1400 series, however, most of them taking little more space than the average secretarial desk. The Houston system also illustrates another growing trend, the interest in turnkey systems developed and offered by commercial firms. The reasons behind this trend area similar to those for networking: they avoid the cost of local systems development, and they eliminate concerns about priority and availability. Presumably they lower the risk of failure, too, since the company supplying the system will normally have undergone a considerable amount of debugging prior to installation.

Commercial systems have had a mixed in library automaton, however. Several large companies have been active for many years in the field, but have been more successful in supplying hardware to libraries than in designing complete systems. Lack of knowledge of the market—in this case, libraries—seems to be the problem, rather then lack of technological capability; systems have been proposed which were based on the company's experience in running its own special libraries, without any apparent realization that larger libraries and libraries of different types have different problems and operate in different ways.

To some extent, the failure of some commercial designs may also be due to the fact that the companies involved are large and have interest in other fields. Similar companies are a different story.

Most of them have concentrated on the library market alone, so they tend to know the market and the business better, but they also tend to be know the market and the business better, but they also tend to be undercapitalized and hence are prone to financial instability. Not a few have gone bankrupts as well as to themselves. Many of the better-run firms seem to have established themselves on a reasonably sound footing, however, and in recent years have made a significant contribution to library automation. Several have offered book catalogues successfully for so many years that the service is now routine, a few have found markets for cataloguing and searching services, and package system companies have been successful in installing dozens of ready-made acquisitions and circulation systems.

The package systems appear to offer numerous advantages. Normally they include all necessary equipment programs, instruction manuals and prepaid training for staff members as well as maintenance contracts and guarantees; in short everything necessary to operate a well-defined area of library operation, such as circulation.

The cost of a library systems staff is thus avoided as in the cost of program development efforts to reach fruition, so common with earlier projects, are also bypassed, and the problems of relations with a central computer do not arise. The problem of overinflated claims, both for operation of the system and service, still makes caution necessary, however, just as caution has always been necessary in the purchase of equipment alone.

An additional cause for caution is that such systems are a relatively recent development and it is just as easy for their designers to underestimate the difficulty of automating library operations as it was for library systems staffs before them. For some types of projects and in some libraries, moreover, a local, in-house effort may continue to be the only feasible alternative, and without continued experimentation little further progress in the field is likely to result.

Commercial firms do have risk capital, however, and most libraries do not, so the availability of well-designed and fully supported commercial systems offers a welcome alternative for library automation to many libraries in the future.Attempts to use such networks cooperative acquisitions are less likely to succeed, and seem destined to fall into disfavour.

Acquisitions work is more likely to be done on commercial package systems development effort of Columbia, Chicago, and Stanford universities found that acquisition procedures differed so widely that a joint effort at systems development in this field was impractical. This situation is unlikely to change in the near future, and local systems will therefore continue to be built, with an increased use of on-line techniques.

Book catalogues will probably remain popular with public libraries where the ease of producing multiple copies makes them particularly attractive, but most of them will come from one of the various commercial book catalogue services rather than from new projects initiated by the libraries themselves.

Academic libraries will continue to use book catalogues to a lesser extent, although the increasing need to share resources and the concomitant need to make existing resources more widely known may lead to a greater use of book catalogues than heretofore.

The management of the actual development and implementation itself rests with library management. Unfortunately, it is a kind of management relatively unfamiliar to the librarian. The work is highly technical issues involved. Furthermore, usually it is a one-time project, rather than an on-going operation such as the library itself represents. As a result, the management problems are very different from those normally encountered in library administration.

The development of a system requires may compromises to be made among conflicting requirements and capabilities. Great care is required to avoid an over-commitment to the demands of one or another specialised interest—to those who regard the aim as effective utilisation of equipment. To those whose concern is with cost/effectiveness, to those concerned with day-to-day operations, to those with some ideal of perfection. A mechanised system will introduce significant changes in the relationships among the library, its staff, and its readers.

The library management must therefore plan a program of education for the staff and public relations with the readers to ensure an understanding of the effects of mechanisation and acceptance of them. Generally, it can be described in this way: Automation of library clerical processes is not a trivial problem even though, superficially, they seem to be little more than analogues of business data processed which have now been computer-based for years.

There are vitally significant differences which must be recognised in management planning. Libraries are concerned with files of truly enormous magnitude.

For example, whereas an inventory control file for a very large company might contain ten million characters, the catalogue of a typical library will contain ten times as much one hundred million characters. That of a large research library will contain over one billion characters, and the National Union Catalogue has been estimated at one hundred billion characters!The conversion of such immense files into machine language is almost prohibitively expensive, but the storage and maintenance of them on a continuing basis is even more expensive. The library data processing involves the very substance of the library's functions. In this respect, the library's catalogue, serial records, and even its circulation control files are comparable to the manufacturing component of a company and not to the bookkeeping records.

Changes in the basic records of the library, which are almost certain to occur with mechanisation, therefore affect the character of the library service themselves and not simply of peripheral accounting procedures. It may be for this reason that library data processing involves a degree of intellectual judgment far beyond that in normal business data processing. For example, catalogue filing rules are with good reason much more complicated than simple alphanumerical sorting.

In fact, in this sense mechanising library data processing is comparable in difficulty and complexity to the development of a total management information system for a company. Library operations and their costs are relatively ill-defined, at least in the form required for mechanisation. Only recently have libraries added systems and procedures personnel to their staffs, and few libraries, even now, have procedures manuals in the detail to be found in a business.

There are still relatively few people available who combine knowledge of libraries with that of data processing. Management planning therefore must recognise the necessity for adequate systems work, including procedures analysis, and accommodate the difficulties in finding or training personnel capable of doing this work. The most important step in the management of a mechanisation program is the definition of objectives for it. Because program objectives must be compatible with library policies, the library administration must being by reviewing existing policies, both as documented and as generally understood. In doing so, it will probably find it necessary to develop some new policies and to document many previously undocumented ones.

Then, the situation which led to the decision to undertake a modernisation program should be analysed. Typically, these might include demands for change coming from higher governing bodies; requirements for new services in response to changing conditions; increasing backlogs due to inadequate budgets, staff, or space. In any case, program objectives must be established which reflect both library policies and current or anticipated needs.

The most ambitious general objective might be the orderly development of a total system which not only exploits as many of the new technologies as possible, but does so with optimum balance of cost and effectiveness and compatibility with other (state, local, or national) library systems. A more limited one might be the documentation and analysis of existing library operations with the aim of limited improvement, through reorganisation or simplification and through limited use of proven equipment techniques and technologies.

Very limited and specific objectives could include faster processing of new book orders, better control over technical processing routines, availability of more comprehensive statistic, better management information, reduction in routines performed by clerical staff, availability of better bibliographic descriptions of the collection, more effective utilisation of professional staff, improved reference services, better control over the physical collection, reduction of patron involvement in the charging transaction, and better circulation control. In defining objectives, the librarian is confronted not only with the uses of cost and effectiveness of services as required now. He should be even more concerned with the quality and quantity of services required in the future.

Will the library, with its present means, be capable of furnishing them? What must be done so that the expected service will be made available? As a result, the librarian must make predictions and projections about the future as well as clearly understand the present roles and purposes of his library. Admittedly, the dynamic development of our educational and cultural system, together with the revolutionary developments experienced by library science in the past few years, all tend to decrease considerably one's confidence in any prediction.

Nevertheless, even poor projections are better than none, and they can be revised often in order to maintain a reasonable, albeit minimal, degree of credibility. For this reason, it is particularly important to develop objectives in terms of a planned progression of systems starting from the present ways of doing things and leading to some ultimates system. The importance of such an approach to library automation should not be underestimated. Libraries, as operational agencies, require that throughout development there be some level of system at all times in regular, full-scale operation in the library.

Even more significant is the necessity that any interim system be capable of sustained, economic operation indefinitely. There is always uncertainty with respect to both the future and the actual progress in development of new systems. For example, related programs elsewhere and the actual availability of technology are completely outside the control of the individual library and yet essential to its planning.

The progression of steps must be designed to articulate well with those programs as they actually develop. Because of these considerations, such a progression should be planned around a logical succession of systems which perform essentially the same functions but at increasing levels of sophistication.

It may therefore frequently be desirable that less sophisticated objectives be met first, as the basis on which later systems are built. Only in this way can the library avoid the pitfalls of over-commitment to some ultimate concept, on the one hand, and of a refusal to proceed on the other. The management planning task, assisted by the library systems analysis staff, is to delineate those functions which are to be served at each stage in the progression.

Some of them will simply be continuations of existing function, unchanged in any substantial way. Others will represent significant changes- such as a book catalogue replacing a card catalogue. Still others will represent totally new services-perhaps mechanised information retrieval or facsimile transmission. And some will represent the need to interface with other libraries.

Criteria used in this planning process include:

— the economic value to be expected from including, changing, or even deleting functions,

— the logical progression in conversion from an existing function to another, more sophisticated one (e.g. in transition from a card catalogue to a computer produced book catalogue to an on-line computer catalogue),

— the need to relate with others in other libraries,

— the availability of budget and personnel,

— the availability and reliability of the necessary hardware and software

— the flexibility and ease of change,

— the consistency with the ultimate objectives.

The process of development and implementation of a mechanised library system is complicated and involves a large number of people. Therefore, the management of this effort must also be planned in advance, the tasks that are to be carried out assigned to development staff, and time estimates established for each task with target dates for their start and finish.

The process of creating any mechanised processing system involves the performance of activities in a series of phases, commonly used in describing and planning computer work in both government and industry. They represent a natural sequence for development of mechanised library systems as well. They are:

— Feasibility analysis.

— Requirements specification.

— Detailed design.

— Computer programming and check-out.

— Computer program functional test.

— Installation and implementation.

— Maintenance.

Feasibility analysis: Based on a statement of the library's requirements, an estimate must be made of the resources required for the project. A summary project plan must be prepared, and a cost-versus-benefits comparison made. During this step, the level of analysis of the library's operating system is only that absolutely necessary for cost estimation and preliminary planning purposes.

Major tasks include:

— Assemble documentation on library policies and practices.

— Determine necessary development activities, including number and identify of any subsidiary efforts.

— Estimate development costs for each step or task.

— Check reasonableness of estimates.

— Perhaps summary budget plan for development.

— Estimate costs of both existing and proposed systems.

— Prepare cost-benefits evaluation of the proposed application.

Requirements specification: This step consist of the detailed study of the existing library system, and the formulation of the operational requirements for the proposed system.

Major tasks include:

— Determine library's system requirements in detail.

— Analyse library's environment including projects with which it must be compatible.

— Determine needed computer program characteristics.

— Prepare performance specifications.

— Assure concurrence of library policy-makers with system performance specifications.

Detailed design: Based on the requirements specification, this step proceeds to the definition of detailed design for both the computer system and the library personnel involved. Major tasks include:

— Interpret requirements specification in terms of specific equipment, volume of activity, response times, and operating environment. Review available software.

— Analyse decision to "make or buy"

— Revise specifications as necessary to conform with decision.

— Produce a system flow diagram.

— Define interfaces with other activities in the library or in other libraries.

— Specify computations, logical manipulations, and transformations within each part of the library function to be done by the machine.

— Design the formats and organisation of all forms and files, including machine stored records.

— Develop requirements for editing, formatting, storing, and updating of the machine stored records.

— Produce documentation of the detailed design.

— Define test requirements.

— Indoctrinate programming personnel.

Computer programming: Based upon the detailed design specifications this step proceeds with all work necessary to produce, document, and test computer programs. Included are such activities as flow charting, coding, integration of individual programs into a program system, preparation of test data bases, detecting and correcting errors, compiling or assembling operating programs, and listing of code. It results in a completed computer program end product, tested for conformity with detailed specification. Major tasks include:

- Flow chart each component computer program.
- Specify all input and output forms.
- Write programs from detailed flow charts or other program design documentation.
- Compile and check program code, and make necessary error corrections.
- Test the performance of each individual program and of the total program system.

Computer program functional test: This step covers demonstration tests of the computer program system, for the library management, usually in a simulated environment at the library. Included is conduct of the demonstration tests and analysis of the rest results. All necessary work to remedy design deficiencies revealed by these tests should be charged to the appropriate previous steps.

The results should be a computer program that is proven to be in conformance with the detailed design specifications and accepted by library management. Major tasks include:

- Conduct test according to plan.
- Analyse test results.
- Initiate any modifications needed for computer programs.
- Document test results.

Installation and implementation: This step covers all work necessary to install the system at the library. It includes training as well as activities for conversation from the existing manual operation. Major tasks include:

— Prepare documentation for library staff.

— Supervise conversion of data required to make system operations.

— Develop training plan for library staff.

— Conduct training program.

Maintenance: System maintenance is required for improving, changing, and correcting operational computer programs. Revisions are need because operations requirements are continually changing during the both the development and operation of the system. Although operational needs are projected during requirements analysis, in most cases they can be neither totally defined nor totally implemented in the imposed time schedules. Corrections must usually be made to the computer programs because errors and operational deficiencies not detected in the routine testing of the programs are usually discovered when the system becomes operational. Much of the work of program maintenance personnel must be devoted to the handling of emergencies; the remainder to modifications required to meet environmental changes. Major tasks include:

— Develop maintenance plan and organisation.

— Provide continuing communication between library operating staff and computer programmers.

— Establish change procedures.

— Process system changes.

During later stages in the planning, all of the specific activities required to accomplish program objectives will be identified as tasks in the work breakdown structure. Each of the tasks may in turn be assigned a cost account number for which funds may be budgeted. The cost account structure is used in implementing cost accounting routines. Each increment of cost is posted periodically against each of the cost account numbers. The individual elements are added together in such a way as to provide cumulative cost records at each of the summary levels in the cost account structure.

At the highest level in the structure the total cumulative cost for the entire program is summarised. This number is plotted on a program status chart and monitored closely by program management. Any significant deviations of actual cost or performance from the planned cost/performance curve is the signal to program management to initiate appropriate corrective action. Among the most important activities which should be included in project planning is the education of both staff and users in the operation, implications, and effects of the system. It is necessary for several reasons.

— Staff are rightly concerned about the effects which automation will have on them personally. Unless they have a sense of involvement, this concern can turn into outright fear and antagonism. A well-planned program of education, scheduled to proceed in parallel with the development project can help overcome this concern.

— The staff will need to change many of the ways in which they have carried out their assigned tasks. Some of those tasks themselves may even change. In principle, the procedures manuals and task descriptions generated as part of the programming work during development are sufficient to show each staff member how work should be performed. In fact, of course, intensive training is usually required, if only to show each person how his work relates top the system as a whole. In this respect, it must be recognised that while automation of clerical processes may not change the basic professional content of librarianship, it will change much of the detail.

— Many times only the staff is really in position to recognise a serious flaw in an operating procedures.

— Any change of system is bound to produce temporary traumas. Failures, changes from the familiar, bruises to aesthetics- all are bruises to occur, if only because something is new.

It must make the staff knowledgeable about what the equipment coming into the library will do and what their own part will be in the new system. Only then will they be willing and able to participate with personal interest in successful operation. Fortunately, time is great factor which contributes to the ease adjustment to the encroachment of the machine.

The library administrator can take advantage of the year or two or even three that the development will require to get his staff actively involved. And this should not be a voluntary involvement, left to the discretion of "interested" personnel, which ignores the very person who most needs to be drawn into the activity. It is especially important to inform staff from the time of their first awareness of the planning for a change in system. The decision to introduce a new system is made only after extensive analysis of the impact which the new equipment and system will have on the library's interests. By the same token, the employee is just as anxious to learn what impact the new system is likely to have on his interests. Frank and open discussions by management are therefore necessary to reduce rumours that otherwise may give a distorted view of the situation.

A well-planned information policy throughout the organisation has advantages even after a commitment is made to obtain equipment. If the introduction of a new system is tactfully presented, it can generate pride and satisfaction in the organisation, but the program should not be oversold or potential difficulties minimised. The important point is the realisation by management that all employees need complete and accurate facts. It should be apparent therefore that an orientation program requires intensive and careful planning comparable to that carried on for the other aspects of the development and installation.

The different requirements of various types of library staff and users for information about the system must be considered. Appropriate techniques must be developed for the dissemination of necessary types of information. Many libraries currently have a book selection which contains principles applicable to nonbook materials. However, to realistically cover all media included in the collection of the resource centre, revision and expansion of an existing policy or adoption of a new one is essential.

For both protection and guidance the statement of policy governing selection must have the sanction of the administration of the institution and of its official controlling body. Perusal of officially adopted statements of other libraries will facilitate the preparation of materials selection policies. These may be general or specific in their coverage. As a rule, they clarify the philosophy and objectives of materials selection and identify both the legal, official entity and the personnel responsible selection and identify criteria for evaluation.

Criteria for special subject areas such as sex, religion, narcotics, and political doctrines, may be stated in detail. In addition, procedures for selection, for gift acceptance, and for handling questioned materials are frequently included.Those responsible for the formulation of the policy will have to assess prevailing conditions in the area served, the temper of the community, the opinions found on the governing board, and previous policies and precedents.

Discriminating choice of audiovisual materials cannot be based on the traditional idea that they are nothing more than handmaidens to the book. They must be clearly and objectively viewed in their own right. Their merits must be evaluated, not in comparison to books and magazines, but in an assessment of their own specific contribution to satisfying the often unexpressed needs of the library public. This revised viewpoint recognizes the shortcomings of a library collection tailored generally to middle class suburbia; its awareness of current changes continuously emphasizes and aggressively seeks service to the individual, whatever may be his intellectual, social or economic situation.

These concepts reaffirm the importance of two familiar and accepted principles considered fundamental in the selection of all types of materials: a comprehensive knowledge of the populace and its desires, and an extensive fund of information on all kinds of resources. Without a knowledge of the materials themselves any attempt to formulate criteria for selection will only lead to confusion. Any set of criteria must have the flexibility to permit common sense adaptations to both specific materials and particular situations.

Rigidity in criteria and literalness in their interpretation can produce both frustration for the librarian and a collection lacking in those elements essential for communication with all individuals and groups. Relevance, as determined by changing conditions and varying audiences, promotes communication, and as such is of basic importance in selection. When the customary evaluation criteria of authenticity, appropriateness, scope, interest, organization, special features, and physical characteristics are seen in the light of such factors as type of library and its desired goals, patron homogeneity or heterogeneity, and availability of materials, their relative importance will vary.

6

Strategic Management of Modern Libraries

Libraries represent long-established and complex arrangements of a variety of formalized modes of access to knowledge. There is a disciplinary continuum between librarianship and information science with no easily identifiable boundary separating them, though the difference between the extreme ends of the continuum are clear and even dramatic.

Librarianship

Librarianship's origins lie close to the origins of writing could be inscribed, and above all to the social and economic pressures that led to the preparation, preservation, and retrieval of permanent written records. These were necessary to processes of stable government and commerce, to organized religions with commonly accepted rituals and beliefs, and to the cumulation and transmission of the knowledge of the times. Thus, we may speak of librarianship in the ancient world as well as in the modern world. Nevertheless, it was not until the last quarter of the nineteenth century that modern librarianship began to emerge as a professional occupation. As such, it was characterized by the invention of tools, techniques, and organizational structures that were widely adopted in the then rapidly multiplying university, college, public, school and special institutional libraries.

Strong formal associations of librarians were created at this time. Indeed, we may date the beginning of the professionalization of modern librarianship as an occupation in the English-speaking world from the foundation of the American Library Association in 1876 and the Library Association of the United Kingdom in 1877.

Among the responsibilities of these associations were the oversight and continuing modification of commonly held beliefs about the goals and functions of various kinds of libraries.

These associations helped provide a context for the emergence of an apparatus of systematic professional communication, regular conferences, journals, a small monographic literature in which knowledge in the field was codified disseminated for use, and made available for public discussion.

Bibliography

Neither libraries not the existing organizations of librarians were able to initiate or even contribute usefully to the study of solutions to certain general bibliographic problems that lay outside the walls of these individual libraries. This was as true in the United Kingdom as in the United States.

Thus, the creation of the Bibliographical Society in 1892 was proposed and discussed at the Library Association meeting in 1891. An issue debated at length was just what the relation of the Bibliographical Society of Chicago, founded in 1899 (to become the American Bibliographical 1904) would be with the American Library Association (ALA); indeed, the fourth general session of the 1902 conference of the ALA was placed "in charge" of the Bibliographical Society of Chicago for a discussion of the founding of a Bibliographical Institute. These several bibliographical societies were interested in bibliography as an intrinsically rewarding area of study that had produced notable achievements in its already distinguished history.

Bibliography as these societies conceived it had broad consequences for scholarship a quite apart from libraries. In England, there was in the early days of the Bibliographical Society the intoxicating idea of such a society creating a great catalog of English literature and preparing a revision and supplement to Hain's *Repertorium Biobliographicum.*

In both England and the United States, membership in these early bibliographical societies comprised, certainly are first, many librarians but also, and perhaps that were communicated to each other at meetings and in the journals of their societies

Gradually, interest in what we would today call general issues of bibliographic control tended to subside in these societies, though never completely in the American Bibliographical Society to be replaced by a scholarly preoccupation with books as physical objects. The history of books, printing and publishing the description of old and rare books, special collections of books and manuscripts, the implications of the physical characteristics of bodices and books for various disciplines, and perhaps above all problems in the transmission of texts, such as the relation of manuscript to printed versions-these gradually became the preoccupation of the members of these societies.

As specializations of a highly technical kind developed, *bibliography* unadorned became too vague, too much a portmanteaus term to be useful. Nowadays, the scholarly activity of bibliography according to particular, perhaps not precisely or consistently distinguished criteria of interest affiliation and technique. Bibliographers asserted the overall independence or their own area of intellectual endeavor in new journals among which *the Library* in Great Britain, the *Papers of the Bibliographical Society of America* in the United State or, later, the *proceedings of the Bibliographical Society of Virginia* are important.Such journals help to define the boundaries between bibliographical scholarship and librarianship, and the continuing existence of the journals asserts their continuing importance and separateness.

The early specialized bibliographical journals very soon abandoned discussions of general library problems and issues and even bibliography itself broadly conceived ; increasingly they reported the narrowly focused and highly specialized scholarship previously described. At the turn of the nineteenth, then, librarianship was differentiated from a certain kind of variously designated bibliographic scholarship, though some librarians have always maintained a close contact with it.

Indeed, nowadays aspects of it are sometimes studied in library schools. Nevertheless, differences in orientation between librarians and bibliographers became clear very early. The professional interests of librarians tended to be of a practical kind, firmly focussed on the functions and operational requirements of libraries, the organizations within which librarians were employed.

Bibliographers, however, tended to be unconstrained by such organizations and cultivated a general academic orientation toward books as complex cultural, intellectual artifacts. This difference in orientation was reflected for example, in this remark made at the time the transformation of the Chicago Bibliographical Society into a national body was contemplated:

> "Only a limited number of librarians of the country are likely to become members of any organization whose aim is other than a purely practical one. It has also been pointed out it would be more difficult if not well high impossible, to bring the scholars of the country into membership in a section of a popular organization like the American Library Association."

Documentation

During the early periods of 20th century in Brussels. Paul Otlet et, al., had founded the International Institute of Bibliography in 1895 to create a universal bibliographical catalog organized on new lines. Eventually Otlet developed his idea of bibliography in a series of now neglected but seminal papers into what the called "documentation"

His concern was not to limit bibliographical control to cataloging books in local institutions, but to find a way of creating a universal index of all documents that constituted records of knowledge; books yes but also parts of books journal articles brochures, industrial catalogs patents, certain kinds of administrative records of governments the archives of municipalities, photographs, post cards, newspapers. The problem was to find out what each contributed to the sum of knowledge, what each contained of potentially useful information., and to express and connect this flexibly creatively to what already existed.

Otlet had a clear idea of what he wanted from libraries in the new bibliographical order he was attempting to create. He believed that if the bibliographical apparatus or equipment of individual libraries actively contribute to the advancement of knowledge.

Otlet wanted libraries to cease being mere depositories and to become vital institutes of documentation providing special information services on all matters of interest to all members of the public who might wish to use them.

He wanted to see all libraries transformed into what he called offices of documentation and these to be jointed together in a national and international system of communication for sharing all existing resources, an international documentary network. He envisaged an important role for microfilm in this.

In the view of Otlet and his colleagues, through general bibliographic organization and control what they tended to designate as the new field of documentation -encompassed traditional librarianship it went far beyond it.

Traditionally, libraries were concerned with only a portion of the documentary record, for documentalists, the whole of the record lay within their scope. The methods to be used to exploit the record, and the institutional settings in which this work could take place, they believed could be more various and innovative than conventional libraries.Librarians reacted to the apparent competition and threat of assimilation by what was much touted as a new discipline essentially by denial.

In continental Europe, just after the first World War, social relations between librarians and documentalists broke down; they have never been fully repaired. In England there was some mild general interest by librarians before the war in continental European documentalists and their work. This became stronger after the war, with the foundation in 1927 of an English member-organization of the international institute of Bibliography: the British Society for International bibliography.

The English special library movement, which culminated in the foundation of the Association of Special libraries and information Bureaus (ASLIB) in 1924, shared many interests with British documentalists, and in 1937, the British Society for international Bibiiography was absorbed by ASLIB. Thus, in England, the documentation and operated quite independently of the more, traditional interests and activities of the Library Association.

Library Science

In USA, dissatisfaction with traditional practices of librarianship led merely to what might be called academic bibliographic scholarship, on the special information the special-library movement with its interest in the special information needs of business and industry. Appalled by the absence of rigorous research useful to libraries C.C. Williamson in 1930 asked

> "Can it be that there are no problems in library service that call for scientific research? Nothing more to learn? No unsolved problems ? "And he quoted and slightly modified John Dewey in describing how a library science might emerge. There is no subject intrinsically marked off,

earmarked so to say, as the content of library science. Any methods and facts and principles from any subject whatsoever that enable the problems of administration and *service* to be dealt with in a bettered way are pertinent... It may be doubted with reference to some aspect or other of library service there is any organized body of knowledge that may not need to be drawn upon to become a source of library science..."

As a result, the idea of a library science dates from the late 1920s and specifically from the founding of the Graduate Library School at the University of Chicago. This is school was established in order to bring the best standards of higher education to bear on the education of librarians and through the introduction of the Ph.D degree and the work of the school's faculty to promote research in the field.

In a statement of policy for the school, Douglas Waples listed what the faculty considered to be the distinctive functions of the school:

1. The most important single responsibility of the school is to meet the standards of scholarship and research maintained by other graduate departments of the university both in the character of work undertaken by the staff and by the research interests of its graduates.
2. The major aim is research, defined as extending the existing body of factual knowledge concerning the values and procedures of libraries and their many aspects, and including the development of methods of investigation whereby significant data are obtained, tested and applied.
3. Not all of the studies undertaken by the school need be confined to research in its restricted meaning of search for abstract principles. In

many instances, they may more properly be called service studies intended to increase the effectiveness of library service.

4. An important function of the schools is the preparation collection and publication of monographs whereby the results of significant studies are made available to the library professions.

A minor classic of librarianship was written by an early member of the faculty of the Graduate Library School Pierce Bulter's *Introduction to Library Science.* Certainly there was an attempt at the Graduate Library School to find new perspectives from which to study libraries and their problems. These perspectives were social sciences and historical scholarship. These methods were introduced to challenge the existing reliance on shared practical experience as the basis for the field's professional knowledge, with all that this reliance implied of a stultifying orthodoxy of dogma and belief.

The importance in the United States of the Graduate Library Schools for the professionalization of-and the appropriate institutionalization of an educational apparatus in the nation's universities for-librarianship has been widely acknowledged. The Graduate Library School embodied what was for a time a unique and controversial approach to professional education its professors and students steadily produced a formidably body of research where before practically none existed. The school issued the first scholarly journal in the field, *The Library Quarterly*; and graduated those who became influential librarians or faculty members in other library schools.

The 1950s saw a fairly rapid increase in doctoral programs. These programs by definition emphasized the importance of research, as opposed to training practitioners, and increased the volume and quality of the fields literature by reporting this research. Thus, the idea of a library science is hardly more than fifty years old, and any great volume or research in the field is relatively recent.

The approach to creating a library science outlined by Williamson some fifty years ago still obtains: It is still to take the substantive problems of libraries and librarianship and apply to them research in the field has employed and continues to employ, the methods of the social science or is historical in nature.

Latterly techniques of systems engineering and mathematical modeling or analysis have proved invaluable in conceptualizing library problems in a new way and providing powerful new techniques for analyzing research data. While the idea of a library science is now widely accepted within the library profession as desirable, it is only a little exaggerated to say that we do not yet have an extensive, distinctive, coherent well-integrated or systematized and scientifically derived body of theoretical and practical knowledge in librarianship.

This leads to criticism of library science as a science and to suspicion of librarianship as a profession. That it is, however, exaggerated should be acknowledged because of the existence of cumulatively important subjects of library literature in the areas, for example, of systems engineering operations research, use and user studies classification and indexing management and measuring effectiveness among others.

Nevertheless, it seems clear to me, despite the research that exists and the academic location of professional education that the empiricism of nineteenth-century librarianship—which the new library science was to test and perhaps ultimately supersede-remains strongly present in the library profession today. That is to say, much of the librarian knowledge continues to be arrived at, and quite generally accepted in a pragmatic way through library practice and the shared experience of librarians.

Our cataloging codes and major classification systems, for example, are of this nature. It is probably true that the central core of knowledge underlying librarianship is still of this empirical kind and that consequently library science has failed to lead to an extensive and solid corpus of objectively derived, systematically examined and accumulated knowledge.

In 1933, Watson Davis proposed that a scientific information institute be set up to help foster communication among scientists and improve existing methods of bibliographical control of scientific literature would, toward these goals especially exploit the developing technology of microphotography. His proposal elicited widespread comment at home and from the European documentalists.

As nothing came of his proposals, he created in 1935 a Documentation Institute within Science Service, an agency for the popularization of science of which he was the director. He used the word documentation to include "all phases of issuance, use and interchange of recorded information." The word attracted him as a term because it had a wide circulation in Europe as a result of the work of Otlet and his documentalist colleagues while having no particular meanings associated with it in the United States.

The American Documentation Institute was created in 1937 as a kind of club to involve-through their directors or other senior officers-a wide range of libraries, learned societies, and government agencies in microfilm and other projects at first insufficiently supported and then more or less repudiated by Science Service.Though founded in 1937, the American Documentation Institute became a professional and scholarly force only with the publication of its journal *American Documentation* in 1950 and with the institute's transformation into a general-membership organization in 1953.

Nevertheless, the early emphasis on technology, scientific communication and publication and new services offered through new kinds of institutions anticipated later developments within the institute. Here essentially, was an attempt, stimulated by technology innovation, to place library and library-related problems in the context of scientific communication. Vernon Tate's editorial description of the scope of *American Documentation* makes it clear that he, like Davis saw the European documentation movement as at last crossing the Atlantic to the United States and from his point of view finding in the journal a vehicle that would ensure its subsequent development.

The journal was to deal with "The totality of documentation," and the definition of documentation given was that which had been accepted, Tata noted by the International Federation for Documentation, for witch the American Documentation refers to the creation, transmission, collection classification, and use of documents may be broadly defined as recorded knowledge in any format." Tate also went on to observe of the new work being done by documentalists: "Traditional methods of communicating and recording knowledge are being studied, reorganized and supplanted and in some cases revolutionized".

The documentalists considered them selves a breed quite apart from librarians. Unlike librarians, they were not documentation from a wide variety of scientific and technical fields. They were responding exuberantly to powerful social forces. As a Jesse Shera has said of this period: "First of all interest in the problem of information on the part of the scientific world and the federal government reached an unprecedented level.

Coupled with this was a period of accelerated technological development." The exploding world of scientific literature; new communications and information processing technology; mammoth programs of governmental research calling fro new systems of information organization storage, and retrieval-these were the winds and waves of these new mariners the documentalists and the information scientists they formally became in 1968, when the American Documentation Institute became the American Society for Information Science. They invented a new language in which to discuss their work. They became increasingly involved with the computer and mathematics.

Machine-stored, manipulated and transmitted data inevitably involved a reassessment of what constituted a document and what documentation was. The computer raised the possibility of a wide range of indexing and retrieval experiments hardly possible before. And, indeed, it may well be that retrieval experiments in the 1960s constitute a first flowering of information science as a science.

Information science as a discipline nourishing certain professional activities developed rapidly in the 1960s. In 1965, the first *Annual Review of information Science and Technology* appeared. It is of particular interest because it represents a relatively early survey of the literature of the field and its segmentation into what appeared at that time to be the accepted major disciplinary components. These components vividly exemplified the importance of the computer in giving shape and direction to both discussion and research in the field. The change of the name of the American Documentation Institute to the American Society for Information Science was intended to reflect the changing orientation of the society's members.

The adsorption of the slippery term information led to many theoretical and frequently tortuous attempts at definitions. During the decades of the 1960s and the 1970s, there was also much discussion about what an ideal curriculum for information science might look like as opposed to those already in existence for librarianship. Many of the developments of the late 1960s may be interpreted as the latest culmination of ongoing attempts to create a more general understanding of how to facilitate access to recorded knowledge than was possible in librarianship, which was perceived as being limited to creating collections of books and related library materials and to managing libraries, or to documentation, which focused on a more abstract notion of records of knowledge or documents.

In its turn, information science represented an approach to an even more abstract level of analysis; it included books and documents while not being limited to them.

Information science has permitted the development of research that is more generally cumulative and generalizable, more readily enriched by importations from other disciplines. It has led to the development of new options, procedures, and organizational arrangements for facilitating access to information recorded, or manipulated, in new ways.

By 1970 this was the situation. On the one hand was a vigorous librarianship, its practitioners still blissful in their relatively undisturbed pragmatism despite the existence of an important scholarly apparatus for the profession involving in part the nation's graduate library schools and despite increasingly lip service to the importance of research for the development of their field.

Their journal and monographic literature has become voluminous though fragmented. They aware organized into a number of large well-established professional associations with a wide range of competing sometimes conflicting, professional functions.

On the other hand was the new, equally vigorous discipline of information science, with a strong research orientation underlying its professional and service components, its own small fairly homogeneous learned society, a generalized field of study (whose precise boundaries, however, were in constant dispute), and a recently established bibliographical and educational apparatus.

Library schools aware of the limitations of library science and recognizing that information science might provide a more respectable disciplinary base for the profession of librarianship enticed or co-opted information scientists as faculty. Or that it was hoped that if a little information science were added to their library studies, library-school graduates might find the job market opening up. Or that information scientists could not really find a more congenial academic home in engineering or computer science or mathematics department than in library schools. There may be some truth in all of these statements

In the 1950s, Jesse Shera and Margaret Egan, Students of the work of Bradford and the European documentalists, in a series of still valuable papers developed new ideas about librarianship, bibliography, and information. They spoke of bibliographic organization. Speculated about classification, sought an intellectual foundation for librarianship and bibliography in a theory of social epistemology, and tried to understand the significance and implications of the rapidly changing information technology of the times.

During his tenure at Western Reserve University and later, Shera was a witty, thoughtful observer of new applications of the computer to information handling. He was a librarian eager to reconcile what seemed necessarily divergent movements; he was a synthesizer, a gadfly, a theoretician. He held librarianship, documentation and information science together intellectually in a broad and scholarly perspective and encouraged their joint institutionalization in the library school at Western Reserve, of which he became dean.

In 1963, Son Swanson, a physicist who had become an information scientist, was appointed dean of the GRADUATE Library School at Chicago. In 1964, he organized the 29th annual conference of the Graduate Library School on the subject of the intellectual foundations of library education. In his introduction to the conference, he observed:

> The fields of information science, information technology, information retrieval and documentation will not be treated as separate topics but rather as an integral part of library science.... thus we shall not be concerned with whether information science is part of library science or vice versa, but rather we shall assume that the educational process in a graduate library school must adequately take both into account. Swanson then went on to

> outline a group of substantive questions that might affect the immediate future of library education and research and that encompassed much of what information dealt with at the time.

These instances and we should stress that many more could be adduced, are of leaders in the field alive to new possibilities. They were indifferent to, or at least undisturbed by, jurisdictional disputes between certain librarians of the time who were fearful of computers and scientific method and some information scientists who were disdainful of the pragmatism and apparent parochialism of librarians. These leaders had a broad generalized perspective that allowed them to discern the general but common problems that underlay librarianship and the new developments in information processing that were sparked by the computer revolution. The computer eventually gave arguments overwhelming force in two ways. Its exploitation in individual libraries led to an almost universal interest of librarians in systems analysis that required identifying and recording library operations at a level of detail appropriate for possible computerization. And this inevitably called into question much of the conventional wisdom underlying library organization and administration.

The development of the Online Computer Library Center and later of other bibliographic utilities and networks and online indexing search services required librarians to move beyond the confines of their own libraries using a sophisticated electronic technology. Moreover, it become clear that problems involved in creating and exploiting these systems both locally and centrally were of a complexity and magnitude and yet of a solvability previously unparalleled in librarianship. Of course, the computer in and of itself was not responsible for these developments.

The exploitation of the computer in developing new institutional relations between libraries and in improving local library processes and procedures was encouraged by the growing volume and complexity of materials that had to be dealt with and by a fiscal plight that has increasingly severe.

Nowadays computer-based systems that have been created as a response to these pressures have become one of the major foci of developments in librarianship. Technical requirements, operational refinement, and improvement of various systems have brought professional librarians and professionally active information scientists together in a way that makes them virtually indistinguishable.

Librarianship as librarianship in this context typically concerns itself with the organizational, political, jurisdictional and economic aspects of the problems that these systems create and to which, in part they attempt to respond.

Developments in Librarianship

Recently, the Library School at the University of Illinois changed its name to Graduate School of Library and information Science. At Denver, the school became the Graduate School of Librarianship and Information Management. At Brigham Young University, the school is called the School Library and Information Sciences. At Berkeley, It is the School of Library and Information Studies, while at Chicago, though a range of information science courses is taught and the school is reported as one of the first to attempt the systematic integration of a library-and-information science curriculum, the school continues to be called the Graduate Library School. Despite these differing appellation, collectively, we still tend to call all of these schools library schools, but that is no longer precisely accurate in teams of their interests and scope and how they wish to present themselves to the rest of academy.

The importance of the name changes lies in what they represent-a shift of emphasis from libraries to something more general. The curriculum in most of these schools now includes courses dealing with computers and computer programming; database creation management, and development; information storage and searching more generally; and behavioral characteristics of various groups and kinds of information producers and users.

The changes in the names of library schools reflect, in part another contemporary trend. The graduates of our library schools as well as becoming librarians now frequently go into information processing or information management, and they are called information specialists, analysis, or constants. This is the second development we wish to mention.

To conventional library jobs, librarians now sometimes add aspects of records management, special indexing services, media management, and research analysis, and they often work in what is called an information center. It has become fairly generally accepted that there is a wide range of professional library and librarylike work that library-school graduates can perform successfully out side conventional library settings.

The next change going to mention is the enormous proliferation of journals in the library and information science fields. Some of these journals have gone through interesting name changes: *Information Storage and Retrieval has become Information Processing and Management; American Documentation* and become the *journal of the American*

Society for Information Science; UNESCO Bulletin for Libraries has become the *UNESCO Journal of Information Science, Librarianship and Archives Administration.* One group of new journals is clearly library related;, *Collection Management. The Serials Librarian, The Behavioral and social Sciences Librarian, Public Library Quarterly, Library Research,* and the *Journal of Academic Librarianship.* Other journals, of no less interest to librarians have in their titles the new language of information work: *On-line Review, Program,* and *Data-Base.* This phenomenon of a rapidly growing number of journals, insofar as it does not represent some from of collective madness, given the economic conditions of the times, must mean something.

We can argue that the phenomenon is, in part the result of the commercial exploration of institutional pressure on librarians and library-school faculty to increase their publishing activities in order to achieve academic and professional respectability. But we may also argue that this literature suggests that a closely related range of subspecializations has developed and, in librarianship especially, achieved a certain maturity-a range that progresses from matters of quite conventional librarianship through key areas in information science.

Journals that tend to draw the boundaries of the fields as a whole, such as the *library Quarterly or the Journal of the American Society for information Science,* include articles, over the whole range of issues and problems dealt with by separate journals, though we assume that there are different frequently distributions of papers across the subspecializations included in the general journals.

Neither the field of librarianship nor information science, given this variety and overlapping of journals, can be perceived as unitary and strictly exclusive of the other. Rather, each is an agglomeration of parts, many of which may be regarded as common to both.

The new language of librarianship is important because it is a terminological reflection of all the changes that have been occurring. It is this body of relatively new terminology that constitutes the fourth change that we wish to identify. Fifteen years ago, when we spoke of a catalog, we meant sometimes a book but usually a card catalog. We looked to the Library of Congress to supply catalog copy in the form of cards or proof sheets. Now we speak, in addition of COM (Computer output Microform) and online public-access catalog, of MARC (Machine Readable Cataloging) data disseminated on magnetic tapes.

In the mid-1960s new technology consisted of keypunch machines, sorters, printers, and a monstrous engine called a computer, to which indirect access was had in batch mode. Nowadays, there is an increasingly large group of librarianships who can speak with some familiarity of CPUs (Central Processing Units) and peripherals; mainframe, mini- and microcomputers; Baud rates and memory capacity; hard discs and floppy disks; and bubble memory.

Reference librarians sensitive to the importance of understanding database structures and search strategies because of new kinds of cost considerations, are expected routinely to conduct what is variously called online or machine-assisted searching of bibliographic and nonbibliographic databases, access to which is purchased from database vendors in dial-up mode using the Tymnet communications systems.

Other librarians buy software and hardware and turnkey systems from commercial censors who are part of something we now designate as the information industry. Once, cooperative schemes led to and reasonably complete only with enormous difficulty and at a prohibitive cost.

Now, we have bibliographic utilities and networks for which the Union Catalog function is but one, and that more or less incidental, of a great range of capabilities. The new language is essentially derived from computer applications in libraries and, as a consequence, is frequently the same as, or at least similar to, that used by information scientists, for whom, historically it can be argued, the computer provided a major disciplinary impetus.

The final development to which we wish to refer is the structural recognition within the formal professional association in both librarianship and information science of major areas of both common and divergent interests. As early as 1951, the Special Libraries Association established a Documentation Division; this division is now the Information Technology Division.

The Special Libraries Associations has a wide range of specific subject divisions and a Publishing Division as well. In 1962 the American Library Association created an Interdivisional Science and automation Division, now the Library and Information Technology Division.

For most of its life, the Resources and Technical Services Division has had a Section for Classification. In 1968, when the American Society for Information Science set up Special Interest Groups (SIGs), one of the first was for Library Automation and Networks and another for Classification Research. Some of the' Special Interest Groups, Particularly in scientific and technical subject areas that are the object of Special Interest Groups have changed, the Library Automation and Network Group and the Classification Research Group have been maintained. Among new groups are those for Community information Services. Computerized Retrievely Services, Nonprint Media and Reprographics, and information Generation and Publishing. These all have counterparts within Library associations.

The Public Library Association of the American Library Association, for example has a Community Information Section; the Reference and Adult Services Division has a Section for Machine Assisted Reference (also called computerized Search Services), the Resources and Technical Services Division has a Reproduction of Library Materials Section; the Library Information Technology Division has sections for information Science and Automation (the old name of the division), audio visual Materials, and Video and Cable Communications.

These all reflected developing areas of mutual interest between librarians as an occupational group and information scientists. The formal associations also reveal areas that do not overlap in so direct or important a way. The differences are clearest where library associations focus on quite specific matters. These are represented structurally within the American Library Association for example, by the type-of-library divisions.

On the other hand, the information science association seems most different when it focuses on information and information processing in a most general way; represented structurally within the American Society for Information Science, for example, by special interest groups on numeric databases, the foundations of information science, and information analysis or evaluation. But librarians increasingly consider that they must be able to use effectively nonbibliographic databases; that the foundations of information science must inevitably encompass recorded information and its "potentiation" for society in organization such as libraries.

Information analysis or evaluation may well deal in a generalized way with issues that a large literate in evaluating library and information services has already attempted to deal with.

Libraries may be regarded as a major institutionalized response to the problems of providing generalized access to the record of what is known. They are a complex organization of access mechanisms. A collection of books and other traditional library materials organized according to the conventions of librarianship by a specially trained and deployed staff for the use of a defined clientele- this is a typical way in which libraries provide access to a portion of the record of knowledge.

The explicit or implicit definition of a clientele provides boundaries as to what will be collected and how what is collected will be organized and made available. In addition, an individual library usually provides a range of staff, a variety of bibliographic and other tools, and creates formalized procedures for gaining both bibliographic access and sometimes physical access to that portion and form of the documentary record that is not directly incorporated into the library. As time has gone by, the ways in which what is known has been recorded, on the one hand, and what constitutes effective access to this record, on the other, have changed.

As well as the variety of forms of printed record there are now other formats in which knowledge or information is recorded; perhaps the latest of these are electronic. Access is required not merely to conventional library materials or to other formats of the record, but to what they contain as well, to their components or elemental parts that can be described as facts, ideas data, information.

In some circumstances, access is provided not merely on demand but in anticipation of demand through selective dissemination of information (SDI) services. Furthermore, access is also seen as increasingly desirable in a limited number of areas of knowledge to the structured content of what has been recorded in these areas. The need to provide this kind of access has led to setting up information analysis centers and social-science-data archives for example, and employing research analysis.

This kind of access has, as a rule, required the participation of kinds of personnel different from those traditionally employed professionally in libraries; special training in the disciplines involved and in computer-based statistical procedures have been thought to be necessary. Schools of library-and-information science nowadays, however, can and do provide some of this training. As the volume complexity, and of formats of the record of knowledge or recorded information have increased and the number of users and the range of potential requirements of access to this record have expanded a variety of responses to these circumstances has occurred.

Some of the responses have been made commercially by what we now call the information industry, which creates and sells bibliographic services and products to libraries, which constitute a major segment of their market, and also independently into an enormously various range of configurations of systems networks, and consortia. Developments in telecommunications capabilities have been seized on as facilitating new kinds of institutional arrangements for providing different levels of access both through libraries and outside of them, as in the experimental home-based VIEWDATA or PRESTEL systems.

New kinds of organizations have been created to provide new kinds of access, such as information centers and data archives. A narrow and conventional definition of a library expresses a limited view of the format of the records involved and modes of access provided to them. But if these limitations are abandoned, libraries may be thought to embrace not only the arrangements and services of traditional libraries but of information centers and data archives as well.

Traditional libraries fall into place on a historical continuum that has arisen as institutionalized responses to the need to provide access to information in recorded form have been developed, examined and modified. Such an approach to a definition may seem to be useful. It includes bookstores and office-filing and records-management systems. It may be argued that it extends to genetics and incorporates museums. While bookstores, office-filing and records—management systems involve what may be described as library like documents, they have in the past tended to fall outside the scope of librarianship. In none of these cases were the systems for, and modes of, access is consummated only on a basis that librarians have tended to repudiate (except in the case of the rental collections some public libraries still maintain the payment of a fee.

Nevertheless, as book jobbers, for example, have developed extensive librarylike systems essentially for the use of libraries, book jobbers have become less hospitals, law firms and other institutional settings, filing and records systems have grown in a scope and complexity and in the sophistication of the technology through which they are maintained, they have began to attract the interest of librarians and information scientists. It is not implausible either to think of a museum as a library of artifacts Suzanne Briet, writing from the point of view of the European documentalists, espouses a definition of documentation almost as broad as this. "An antelope that has been 'cataloged' [in a zoo] is a primary document and other documents are secondary and derivative."

It seems more clearly figurative to speak of chromosomes as libraries of genetic information: Certainly neither man or nature promises generalized access to the information they contain, despite the advances that have been made in genetic engineering. But it at this point of seeking appropriate definitions for libraries, documentation and information science and of exploring their ramifications that we may suggest the continued relevance of the historical development explored earlier by asking the question: What are the phenomena that information science studies ?

Information as electrical impulses in the brain or as represented by certain biochemical phenomena or as the content of disciplines-this set of different meanings raises a serious problem of disciplinary encroachment. When is *information* science information science and not epistemology, psychology, biopsychology. Thus, an ultimate consequence of the process of seeking an ever more general perspective for information science, for the problems of access to recorded and potentially consultable or public information underlying the certain and development of libraries, may be the loss of all sense of disciplinary coherence in the field.

We might argue from the point of view of the continue we described earlier that at one end is the librarian constructing a catalog of books; at the other, because of the way in which information can now be conceived is the genetic engineer consulting the information recorded in and then restructuring DNA. Perhaps, however, there is a discontinuity between the two involving notions of symbolic representation and public consolation that more careful analysis and definition would reveal. The point here is not so much the difficulty of definition or the slipperiness of terminology as the implication that the generalizing process described early in this paper may still be at work. It is a source of innovation and strength but it blurs traditional distinctions and can unsettle professional convictions.

Librarianship is an ancient profession, as old as Babylon. But the government of society and its commerce has depended on the collection and use of information for just as long-from Babylon through the Domesday Book to the United States Census and beyond. Is not then information science equally ancient? We known about the Babylonian libraries by their catalog; we know about the use of information in government and commerce from the existence of inventories.

The principal characterizing principle of the organization of information seems to be list-making that is, we might say that the kind of list-making characterizes the kind of general information activity. Rayward quite rightly described the recent convergence of hitherto disparate disciplines or practices, but in referring to library and information science and bibliographers and documentalists, he seems to present a picture that does not always do justice to the complexity of the nature of the component forces. Further, his historical backdrop, with 1876 as the beginning of formal librarianship and the founding of the Graduate Library School in Chicago as the beginning of research in library science, does not really allow a large enough stage to accommodate the true range of significant characters. In short, while we agree with Rayward's general thesis, we would like to extend it, with reference to some earlier history and other phenomena in the last century. We would like to begin by making a few formal points. Scientists in the late nineteenth century quite outside either bibliographic or library traditions were already coupling indexes and catalogs of scientific materials, because neither librarians nor bibliographers provided them.

From the eighteenth century onward, new libraries and new library practices veered between the bibliographic and documentalist traditions, as they tried, on the one hand, to be scholarly in their catalog descriptions and, on the other, to provide easily used "finding-tools" for their patrons. Rayward is quite right when he says that "[librarianship's] origins lie close to the origins of writing." However, we should remember that the earliest writings were inventories-of property, goods and laws in Babylon, Mycenae, and so forth. Early library catalog of Callimachus.

Similarly, in the Middle Ages, Monasteries kept inventories of their collections and sometimes used them as catalogs. Even as late as the end of the eighteenth century, libraries kept an internal inventory and perhaps an internal slip catalog arranged by author/title and occasionally published a meager author/title entry catalog for the library patrons.

Between 1667 and 1840, even Harward college produced a public catalog only three times. The library catalog as we know it was really the product of the book trade: Aldus Manutius and his contemporaries in the late fifteenth century for bibliographic description: Andrew Maunsell and the English booksellers of the early seventeenth century for the subject catalog: and the early eighteenth-century Paris booksellers like Marchand and Brunet, for the idea of a general bibliographic classification. We should not assume, however, that booksellers gave rise to the bibliographic tradition. Their aim was to sell books which they did successfully by grouping similar books and subjects together in their catalog and describing them explicitly and practically to their customers. On the other hand the classical bibliographer's delight is to record the diversity and differences of books in order to identity individual copies. Indeed, Rayward says,

> "These several bibliographical societies were interested in bibliography as an intrinsically regarding area of study that had:....broad consequences for scholarship quite apart from libraries."

Of course they were interested -the eighteenth century had been a century·of gentleman's individual scholarship. Now there was a hope of institutionalism-perhaps even a society like the Royal Society.

Rayward asserts that

> "we may date the beginning of......modern librarianship.......in the English-speaking world from the foundation of the American Library Association (ALA) in 1876 and the Library Association (of the United Kingdom) in 1877.... But within a generation it become clear that neither libraries nor the existing organizations of librarians were able to initiate or even contribute usefully to the study of solutions to certain general bibliographic problems that lay outside the walls of these individual libraries. This was as true in the United Kingdom as in

the United States."

This is an almost Hegelian interpretation of library history. For the American Library Association to be formed in 1876 meant the coming together of a large number of like-mined professionals. What had Charles Jewett, Charles Cutter, Justin Winsor, and Melcil Dewey been doing in the years before 1876? What had Edwards. Antonio Panizzi, and Andrea Crestadoro been doing in England before 1877? Britain had passed a Public Libraries Act nearly thirty years before.

The years 1876/1877 do not mark the beginning of librarianship they mark its formalizational conference of 1877 was a declaration of the existence of a solid body of knowledge and experience. Jewett had already laid out in the 1840s the three factors essential for solving the problem of universal bibliography: access to material, reproduction technology, and consistent descriptive practice. Jewett, and later, Dewey and Cutter, tried to solve the problem from within the library world, Rayward ignores the very real efforts made towards the standardization of bibliographic description by librarians like Panizzi: Jewett. Cutter, and others.

Conventional libraries did not produce a solution to general bibliographic problems in the last quarter of the nineteenth century-nor did bibliographers. The reason was not a failure due to any one part of our general profession but the effect of historical development-Jewett's three problems were never all solved satisfactorily at the same time. Indeed, as the bibliographers delved even more into the scholarly minutiae of the differences between copies of early printed books, they inhibited the production of large-scale scholarly catalogs. It fell to the very different documentalists (sometimes called scientific bibliographers to add to the confusion) to try to collect and organize all the citations in the scientific literature. Bibliographic control never been a central interest of classifical bibliography.

Classical bibliographers are concerned with differences between copies of a published work. Whereas librarians are concerned with similarities in order to collect them into subject groups on shelves and into author/title and subject groups in catalogs and indexes. Documentalists have librarylike techniques to organize their material. They are on the other side of the librarian from the bibliographer but perhaps not so far away. As Rayward says,

> In the view of Otlet and his colleagues, though general bibliographic organization and control-what they to designate as the new field of documentation encompassed traditional librarianship, it went far beyond it. Traditionally, libraries were concerned with only a portion of the documentary record; for the documentalists, the whole of the record lay within their scope.

Although Otlet certainly addressed general bibliographic control in 1895, so had Melvil Dewey, as evidenced in the preface to the first edition of his classification scheme in 1876. Actually the problem had been that librarians, influenced by classical bibliographers, wanted to include a kind of formalized record in the manner of the bibliographers.

This had begun under the influence of Panizzi's cry for " a full and accurate catalog" and, by 1908, with the joint Anglo-American code, was somewhat divorced from the indexing tradition of Pool's *Index*, and so forth. Early documentalists wanted comprehensive coverage, sufficient (i.e., perhaps minimum) record, and precise location. Unfortunately, in his discussion of library science, Rayward neglects special libraries, the true inheritors of the documentalists tradition. In the United Kingdom at least, in the 1930s/1930s (precisely the period Rayward addresses), there were strong forces binding together the disparate elements of scientific and technological information and formal (mostly public and special) libraries.

Regional networks like Sheffield Interchange Organization (SINTO), Liverpool and District Scientific, Industrial, and Research Libraries Advisory Council (LADSIRLAC), and so forth, were based in public libraries (with the public library seen as kind of honest broker) and linked all kinds of library and information units for the exchange of nonbibliographic as well as bibliographic information.

To understand the true significance of these networks, and the position of the public library within them, the reader should realize that for at least the first half of this century, public libraries profession. It was not unusual to find city reference libraries richer in their collections and more active in their reference service than university libraries in the same cities. Rayward's suggestion that the formation of a theory of librarianship and library research began with the founding of the Graduate Library School in Chicago seems less cause and effect than a *post hoc ergo propeter hoc* argument.

There had been many scholars, thinkers, and workers concerned with many aspects of library science between 1840 and 1940 most of whom owed no debt to the Graduate Library School. It is true Jewett, Cutter, Bliss Sayers, and Ranganathan addressed individual aspects (although Cutter and Rangnanthan came close to addressing the whole field). It is probably true to say that they did not develop a theory of librarianship but we wonder if one has ever been enunciated. It is true also that much of the work in the late nineteenth century addressed practical aspects of library science—but there are many fields in which research customarily addresses practical aspects of the discipline. We have mixed feelings about attitudes towards or definitions of research especially in library-and-information science.

Library and information science is in an uncomfortable position vis-a-vis research fro two reasons: The discipline is structural rather than substantive and (partly for this reason and partly for historical reasons), it never amassed, or had time to amass, a solid quantitative base of empirical observations in a period of its development early enough to avoid doubts being cast on that kind of research or observation.

Librarians and information scientists very soon found themselves alongside researchers in other disciplines who had that quantitative base and who were now exploring theoretical implications. The profession may do itself a disservice if it seeks to emphasize only "respectable" research.

Rayward alludes somewhat disparagingly to the empiricism of the nineteenth century-yet, like medicine and law, we are profession with a job to do. We hope to improve by learning from research, but we can also improve through carefully considered practice. The best hope we have is precisely the tenor of Rayward's paper: That we are now seeing the convergence of closely related of knowledge and practice that for long, like siblings with territorial problems, have viewed each other at best with suspicion and at worst with outright paranoia. Information has already become the late twentieth century's biggest industry. With a clear view of the nature, origin and potential of the components (that may include ourselves), we may see our way to the best resolution. We believe that this curiosity accounted for the unexpected popularity of Wiener's highly technical Cybernetics and the enthusiastic reception of the mathematical theory of communication.

Program-steered electronic computers, which made their appearance as practical device about that time also. Were enormous potential as logical, symbol processing information engines. Their enormous potential or revolutionizing our conceptions of problem-solving and information-processing also stimulated a great deal of speculation research.It is fruitless to engage in semantic disputes over when a discipline of information is not epistemology, psychology, biopsychology, and so forth. What matters is that investigators who identity with the information disciplines formulate researchable problems and make discovers, and contribute insights that clarify the nature and dynamic of information and knowledge.

Their identification with a scientific community that calls itself information science may, presumably, provide them with ideas, methods, paradigms, and interactions. It may lead to success in ways that have not succeeded in other communities of inquiry. To suggest that the primary focus of information science should be library and information work is stifling and unproductively restrictive. It is not likely to attract scientists in other areas.

The conceptualization of information as the reduction of uncertainly by a receiver about which message, from an ensemble of messages, was transmitted over a noisy transformation of uncertainty with entropy, and claude shannon's theorem about the existence of codes that make it possible to transmit information at rates that come arbitrarily close to a specified upper limit with arbitrarily low probabilities of undetected error, rooted what others called information theory firmly as an engineering discipline. It placed information, in its technical sense, it was definitely divorced from meaning and the less precise interpretations that could connect it to uses such as information in books or documents.Shortly after large-scale computers began to challenge the talents of engineers, mathematicians, and others-those who later called themselves computer scientists-to explore and realize their potential, information retrieval become one of the first application areas.

It was a solution in search of a problem, motivated by the urge to explore all possible uses of computers. It required a broadening of the information concept to include its semantic, pragmatic, and syntactic aspects.

Very few of these precomputer scientists/ engineers were affiliated with the American Documentation Institute (ADI) in the mid-1950s. Taffee T. Tanimoto and Hands peter Luhn were the exceptions, and many of the early pioneers, such as Calvin C. Mooers, still are not active in the American Society for information Science (ASIS), the present name of ADI. It was during the discussion in 1960-1962 about these potential functions of an automated Library of Congress that the idea of a continually updated, on-line encyclopedia like knowledge-base occurred to me. Herbert Bohnert pointed me to H.G.Wells's 1936 world to vannevar Bush, Alvin Weinberg, Watson Davis, and charles Van then in force. These priorities had stressed improved general access to the record of knowledge by specialists.

The needs of our age intersected with the potentials of emerging information technologies in stressing screening, evaluation, and synthesis of what is known and ensuring that continual additions to knowledge fit in to a coherent image that can be brought to bear on the day-to-day problems of all people.

Such services are active rather than only passive. They intervene when intervention is needed. The new priorities stressed a kind of system that primarily teaches, is a work of electronic art, espouses a human viewpoint, addresses and arouses the curious a average person, stimulates his or her curiosity, and aims to improve the world. Only secondarily does such a system seek to inform, perform a reference function, aim at the specialist, and accurately reflect the knowledge, opinions, prejudices of the time.

The proposed system, now called WISDOM (Worldwide Information Service for the Development of Omniscience in Man), is still an idea though pilot versions have been implemented. As a system, it is a social organ that is eventually to supplant the minds of individuals, a kind of community mind that may be the next stage in the evolution do mind.

But WISDOM is also an emerging movement for the previously mentioned reversal of priorities, and several organizations have been created to further his movement.Paul Otlet may have a similar vision in 1895. Indeed, some documentalists and information scientists, such as Eugene Garfield, embraced variants of the idea underlying WISDOM in independent discovery. Which led to contributions of revolutionary impact, such as citation indexing and clusters based on coupling profiles (bibliographic coupling plus cocitation coupling).

Such techniques apply not only to documents that comprise the written record but also to the individuals who use knowledge as well as to the fields of knowledge themselves that are only partially embodied in the records.Librarianship, library science, documentation, bibliography, and information science in the narrow sense used by Rayward, have in common a focus on the written record and the physical documents-books, journals, manuscripts, musical sources, prints and so forth-that it comprises. Librarians are concerned with organizing collecting of such documents and facilitating their use by library patrons. As such, they need to cope with at least three tasks:

1. Continually selecting from the growing record what to collect (possibly wedding little used items to make room if there are space limitations)
2. Bibliographic control or organizing and maintaining the collections as well as maintaining the tools enabling them and their partons to determine at any time what is in the use of records in the library's collection.

Information science, in the broader sense in which we interpret it, is in contrast, concerned with information, knowledge, understanding, and wisdom. Here, information is used in its technical to remove a receiver's uncertainty about an ensemble. It is both a flow and a pattern that flows over a channel. This channel may have a memory that stores the encoded information pattern of bits as meaningless codes. The channel may contain a transducer and transformation that rearrange, encode, decode, or otherwise process patterns of bits, as in a computer.

As a flow, information is a temporal change in a pattern. To be informed is to experience a change in some connective structure; to inform such an experience. Information becomes knowledge when it is given meaning, usually by a human mind. A person (or machine) may be said to know the answer to a previously unencountered question that is not merely a syntatic transformation of the statement troughs which that knowledge was acquired.

Knowing something requires the existences of a knowledge space containing niches for concepts, ideas, d so forth, that are acquired. These niches are organized in to a web, and the way a niche is embedded into this structure, relating it directly to many other niches and indirectly to many more, is what gives it meaning at any time. Knowledge is stock; it may accumulate, but mere accumulation of knowledge is neither understanding nor wisdom. It is the latter that can help us to survive and learn to improve our lives. Knowledge becomes understanding when it contributes to change in a knowledge space, adding new connecting among niches and new niches, perhaps revising the entire or large parts of the structure.

Certain new items of knowledge enable the knower to think of and questions never thought of before is needed. Understanding leads to deeper answers to questions regarding how and why, while knowledge is mostly know-what and know-how. Wisdom, in one sense the ultimate purpose of our intellect and the scientific enterprise, and therefore of central concern to information disciplines, means bringing knowledge and understanding to beat on shaping our world for human ends by human means. Wisdom governs communications of information for purpose of control.

It includes know-when, that is the choice of strategy times for action based on or justified by knowledge and understanding. Clearly, this emphasis is far from concern with access to the written records and even further from understanding is certainly necessary but it is far from sufficient as a profession and scientific foundation for the knowledge industries.

The convergence hoped for by Rayward is certainly desirable, but it is not feasible so long as schools of library science take an attitude of the expressed in the following quotation from a resolution by the faculty of a schools of library science: In its Standards for Accreditation, 1972, the American Library Association's Committee on Accreditation (ALA/COA is the only group which the Council on Postsecondary Accreditation [COPA] recognize for purposes of accreditation in librarianship) defines libraries and librarianship in the "broadest sense as encompassing the relevant concepts of information science and documentation, including "media centers, educational resource centers, information, documentation, and referral centers"...The schools is now actively looking in to additional means of enhancing the information science aspects of the AMLS program. These are parts of a resolution passed unanimously by the faculty of the school of Library Science at the University of Michigan on October 19, 1978, in formal opposition to informal suggestions for establishing a campus-wide doctoral program in the information disciplines with the broader and deeper interpretation sketched here. In doing this, the faculty erroneously judged my interpretation of information science to be consonant with erroneously judged my interpretation of information science to be consonant with that of the Council on Postsecondary Accreditation and the American Library Association's Committee on Accreditation. Note also the phrase "information science aspect of the ALMS program."

An exceedingly narrow topic of the confusion generated by superficial interpretations of "information science and documentation" in its popular sense and with reference to such institutions as libraries or media centers. It is also the typical defensive response of an institution that feels threatened with extinction. Whether that fear is justified or paranoid depends on the ability of such institutions to adapt, as in the case of the Baxter Schools of Library and Information Science are Case Western Reserve university.

The present state in the development of the five fields under discussion is characterized by strongly divergent orientations to information science. Mine differs greatly from the library and information science in the title of Rayward's paper. We may have been among the first to use the term information science in the previously mentioned broader sense.

It may be true that many information scientists, however they interpret their field, found welcome homes in library schools. Librarians and Library Association are full of vitality and excitement. Their hospitality to, and acceptance of, information scientists should certainly be gratefully even if their are barriers to understanding and attitude. If people trained in physical science do not borrow models and paradigms from their colleagues in librarianship, library science, documentations, or bibliography, then this is reciprocated.

A recent survey of librarian's attitudes toward technology showed that they like technologies but not technologists. The forces leading to this state were the relatively slow rate of progress in basic information science, the correspondingly slow development work in the field, the slow growth of the American society for Information Science, the expanding need for graduates of library schools during the 1960s, and the need to adapt to new technologies and new ways of thinking. These forces have now subsided. Replacing them is the more rigorous development of database-management systems, expert-knowledge systems, the use of distributed networks and parallel arrays by computer scientists. Graduates of library schools are no longer in great demand; public libraries, competing for increasingly scarce municipal funds with police, fire, and other vital services, are not receiving enough support to stay even, much less keep up with the growth of the written record at inflated prices.

Publishers can no longer count on libraries who support library schools are demanding that graduates be trained in wholly new ways-with stress on the broader interpretation of information science, and some even request that library be entirely deleted from the name of the degree. The trend is almost certainly away from access to such physical items as printed paper or microforms and away from emphasis on bibliographic control of a physical inventory. Printed paper will probably continue to coexist with alternative forms of recorded knowledge but lose its predominance. We can no longer refer to electronically recorded databases as the written records except in a most general sense.

To be sure, it is as necessary to organize knowledge in the newer recorder from as it is in traditional forms, but the principals of cataloging or indexing taught in library schools may no longer apply. Attention will, we hope, shift to key problems in information science, and their contributions will lead to vigorous enterprise offering new products and services that meet the needs of knowledge-based societies.

When the growing demand for a firm professional and scientific foundation underlying the information sectors of such societies is recognized, those engaged in information will occupy numerous and leading roles and contribute to increasing the productivity of those sectors.

Boyd Rayward has written an excellent general statement, well documented, of the historical development of Librarianship in relation to the emergence of the historical development of librarianship in relation to the emergence of document and the transformation of the latter in to information science.

We shall not deal with stubborn problem of what constitute a disciplinary relation between librarianship and information science until a decision has been reached as to whether these areas of activity are, in themselves, true discipline, we did so mainly because we did not know how else to classify what libertines do and the technologies by which they have striven to achieve their ends.

Information science has yet to prove itself as a discipline. Like librarianship, it is still largely an agglomeration of technologies drawn from other areas of study, particularly, in the case of information science, from mathematics and electrical engineering. In the final analysis, we are still compelled to say, that librarianship is what librarianship is a service and information science is an area of accuracy that

Librarianship is a service and information science is an area inquiry that seeks to measure and improve the efficiency of the librarian: but such as statement is inadequate because information science deals with only a part of what the librarian does. Viewed from the perspective of history, then, as admirably presented by Rayward, Paul Otlet and his associates who formed the Brussels Institute and subsequently the International Federation for Documentation (FID), were basically librarians.

Librarianship has always been interdisciplinary in that its goal was to make the total record of the human adventure readily accessible to all. Otlet and his follows merely strove to expand the area of library activity to encompass a wider range of materials and improve access to those records by using a new technology. They adopted the classification scheme devise by Melvil Dewey to form the Universal Decimal Classification (UDC) and supplemented it by using certain sings and symbols of interdisciplinary relations.

Neither traditional librarians nor these innovators exemplified a new field of academic endeavor; both were essentially centripetal-drawing to themselves the products of scholarship and the accumulated recorded knowledge of many fields. Thus, they pioneers relied on librarianship for their basic principles and structures. They elaborated what had already been done. That they called themselves documentalists and their fields.

Thus, these pioneers relied on Librarianship for their basic principles and structures. They elaborated what had already been done. That they called themselves documentalists and their field of activity documentation did not change their basic objectives. When the documentation movement came to the united states, American librarians rejected the UDC even thought it was based on Dewey's system, because they believed it to be too complex; they turned, instead, to microphotography as a technology that would improve the accessibility and availability of graphic records as well as provide a substantial reduction in costs.

Librarians even foresaw a time when microfilm would replace the conventional book. On this side of the Atlantic, documentalists were mainly librarian who had adopted a new technology; they was no alteration in the basic goals. Because these American documentalists, most of whom were librarians, based their technology on the science of photography, they tended to regard themselves as scientists, tended to avoid the term librarian, and formed the American Documentation Institute (ADI). Thus began the fragmentation that has plagued librarianship ever since.

By mid-century, microphotography had become firmly established as an important addition to the librarian's arsenal of technologies, and most of the members of the American Documentation Institute had turned to other interests. Those few who retained their concern for the further development of microphotography seceded to form the National Microfilm Association, composed mainly of commercial interests organized for the promotion and manufacture of photographic equipment.

The remaining members of the ADI turned to new techniques for the organization of library materials-which they characterized as information retrieval. These new interests were largely devoted to the application of electronic and mechanical systems for improving the accessibility of graphic records. Thus, there evolved such systems and mechanisms as Calvin Mooers's Zato coding, Mortimer Taube's coordinate indexing, Raplh Shaw's rapid selector, and the searching selector fabricated by J.W. Perry and Allen Kent at Western Reserve University.

The ADI was then largely composed of librarians, with the additions of a number of commercial organization, such as Eastman Kodak, Remington Rand and General Electric, which had research resources far beyond those of librarians.

The line of demarcation between documentalists and librarians was even then beginning to be drawn, and there were some suggestions that library schools should changes their names to schools of documentation. Librarianship was becoming a tarnished word, and may wanted to dissociates themselves from it as much as possible.

This movement was intensified by the influence of Claude Shannon and warren Weaver and their work at the Bell Telephone Laboratories on the communication of information.

The term information was misleading, but it was used by members of the American Documentation Institute as being descriptive of their major concern. Again, the influence of Shannon and Weaver became prominent in attracting mathematicians to their field, creating such technologies as bibliometrics and citation analysis. These phenomena had long been known to librarians, but their rebirth gave the phenomenon air of novelty and innovation.

By the late 1960s, the term documentation had become old hat, and the ADI changed its name to the American Society for Information Science. Today, even the special Libraries Association, founded in 1909 by John Cotton Dana (librarian of the Newark, New Jersey public Library) to serve the bibliographic needs of business and industry, is contemplating a change of name to something akin to an association of information managers.

The flight from library goes on, leaving the old and respected name to typify, in the main, public library service. The trend would make an interesting science is rooted in attempts to extend the boundaries of libraries technology and give it revived respectability by endowing it with a unique name.

The American Society for Information Science and its preceding organization, the American Documentation Institute, could provide an excellent subject for the study of that peculiar amalgam that is librarianship information science. Unfortunately, a thorough inquiry of this kind has not yet been made.

However, in 1979, Donald W.King and two graduate students at the library school at Drexel University interrogated the entire membership of ASIS in an attempt to provide a profile of the membership of that organization. The study does provide some interesting insights.

Of the 3894 regular members of the association, 52 per cent responded. Of the responded. Of the respondents, 24.2 per cent, the largest groups was 20.3 per cent, composed of managers, directors, or coordinations. Information technologists, analysts, and scientists came third, with 18.6 per cent, at which point the percentages drop off sharply.

In the survey of the primary employers of ASIS members, 35.6 per cent were from industry, 26.9 per cent were from colleges or universities, and 12.1 per cent were from the federal government. In the sample, 56 per cent were woman, while in the earlier ADI yeas, there was no more than a handful of woman.

Whether or not these statistic reflect the actual situation is problematical in that women may be more responsive to questionnaires of interest to woman. In an editorial on the study, Donald King points out that ASIS members are concerned with four primary professional areas; operational information functions, including searching, preparing, and analyzing data on behalf of others-1490 ASIS members; management of information operations, programs, services, or databases-1160 members; information science and technology, including research and development, systems analysis, and systems design-530 members; and educating or training information professionals or other workers-360 members.

We somewhat glibly assert that librarianship is a field of practice whereas information science is an area of research-and it was in the early days. But today, if the membership of ASIS is indicative, information science is approaching an area of survive not unlike that of librarianship.

Both activities are concerned with the transfer. Information science, however, gets bigger headlines because of its use of engineering and mathematics in its technology. Rayward evinces a certain doubt in his own mind about an organic interdisciplinary between librarianship and information science. Thus, he writes:

> "when, however, the focus becomes not library and information work, but information science, the clarity, such as it is, is lost... [Immediately there arises the] problems of disciplinary encroachment. When is information science and not epistemology, biopsychology. Physiology or physics or journalism or the sociology of groups or anthropology?"

The enthusiasm with which many librarians, especially academic librarians, rushed to embrace new technology with only the most causal consideration of their appropriateness seemed to substantiate Kaplan's "Law of the Instrument". Simply stated, this so-called law holds that peoples tend to formulates their problems in such a way as to make as to make it seem that the solution to the problems demands precisely what they happen to have at hand. He illustrates this law by saying that a small boy given a hammer immediately concludes that everything needs pounding. A more sophisticated example might be that an executive who has acquired photocopying machine almost inevitably concludes that all of his or her immortal prose should be distributed throughout the organization in multiple copies. There are times when it seems that the goal of science is not to know or to understand but to use. In the American character, they has been a strong strain of utilitarianism, or, rather, pragmatism, and this is perhaps no more clearly evident than in Librarianship.

The major figures in the history of American librarianship were doers rather than thinkers; they were concerned with process rather than purpose. They devised and taught in their library schools routines and procedures, and with the advent of in-line networks and access to data bankers, they are doing it more than ever today.

We need not be surprised, therefore, that librarians rushed to embraces science and began to talk glibly science, turning their backs on the library's humanistic origins. Librarians even went so far as to evolve a new discipline called informations science. They misinterpreted shannon and waver's specialized use of the noun information and assumed that it related to the communication of knowledge rather than the transmission of signals.

Information theory, in contrast to the theory of librarianship, is severely limited in its communicative potential to the theory of librarianship, is severely limited in its communicative potential. It is objective is to provide the librarian with a system giving functional or operational access to the contents of documents, Information scientists give all of their attention to design, production, implementation and control of the system.

Thus, as H.Curtis Wright has so well pointed out. Our schools of library science are busily engaged in producting "control artists", technicians and mechanics who tinker with information systems but there are unable to solve problems of access and retrieval because they cannot control ideas. These control artists constantly mistake the symbol for reality and believe that continuing or figuring with these symbols solves the bibliographic access problems. This confusion between data and ideas lead to the confusion between data system and idea systems. Thus, wright is close to what Robert fair throne has called "making and parking" in document retrieval rather than information or knowledge retrieval.

Librarians have becomes so concerned with process that they have confused substance with instrumentation. Processing data canoe performed by machine, but only the human mind can process knowledge or even information.

Information science is based on data and their manipulation, not on ideas. Science deals with things, things that can be measured weighted, poured, fastened, or mixed together, whereas librarians are dealings only incidentally with things but primarily with ideas, concepts, and thoughts. Librarians are, or should be, characterized by their knowledge, not by their instrumentation.

We conventionally say that the computer is here to stay and we must learn to adapt to its powers and capabilities. We submit that the situation is quite the reverse.

The computer is here to stay, therefore it must be made to adapt to the librarian's problems and needs. It must be kept in its proper place as a tool and a slave, or we will become sorcerer's apprentice, with data everywhere and not a thought to think.

Librarians, ever sensitive to the somewhat meager social esteem accorded their activities, devised the term library science and eagerly seed information science as potential supports to their claims to professionalism. But science does not a profession make, and an overlay of scientific operations is not a sine qua non for professionalism.

The term profession derives, of course, from the root verb to profess, to believe in, and etymological, a professor is one who acts according to his or her beliefs or convictions. Wright has recently reviewed the development of the concept from the Greek arete, which meant skill or proficiency in a particular job and a knowledge of the job in hand, to the well-known characteristics of a profession as enunciated by Abraham Flexner.

Wright cites Socrates to the effect that if we wish to know what a good shoemaker, the first essential is to know what a good shoemaker is and what the purpose of the shoe are. Only then can we decide what materials are best for making shoes and what tools should be employed and the best techniques and methods for using these materials and tools. But such skill and techniques cannot be successful without an understanding of what is to be produced and what functions it is supposed to perform.

Wright quite properly sees a direct connection between knowledge of a task and it is performance, citing the so-called Socratic Paradox that "Virtue is knowledge". Which was interpreted by his contemporaries to mean that we cannot be efficient unless we take the trouble to learn our job.

Stripped of the verbiage that has accumulated around the paradox over the centuries, what Socrates meant was that when there is a specific occupational function to perform, the worker must perform that function knowing what the task is, what its purpose is, and the best way of performing it. This, says Wright, is the true basis of professionalism.

We might also cite the statement attributed to Michelangelo, that the apprentice sculptor should learn anatomy thoroughly and then forget it. By this admonition, he enunciated the belief that a piece of sculpture should not do violence to an batomical laws, but, at the same time, it should be more than an exercise in anatomy. He was subordinating process to purpose.

Librarians would do well to remember occasionally Moses or a pieta and think somewhat less frequently of shannon and Weaver. What, then, is the "shoe" that is the end product of the 'shoemaker" the professional librarian. We submit that there are three components in the concept of a library.

First, there is acquisition, which involves knowing what to a acquire for a given clientele and how to acquire it. Acquisition implies substantive knowledge of the materials and the uses to which that knowledge can and should be put.

The second is organization, that is, ways in which the accumulated materials can be arranged and processed for maximum convenience and efficiency of use. It is here, and only here, that information science makes its contribution to librarianship. The theirs is interpretation and service, which is the reason deter of the library, and it is here that information science reveals its greatest threat of dehumanizing the library's function.

To express the same idea in another way, the library can be seen as three interrelated spheres: the sphere of optimum content; the operational or mechanistic sphere; and the sphere of maximum context. If librarians parasites in sublimating librarianship to the lure of the machine and the all importance of data retrieval their "shoes" will be very uncomfortable to the user, and they will leak at certain vital points. Jeans-like the library looks in two directories simultaneously. It looks towards the social science, because it is a creature of society, evolved to meet the needs of human beings working towards the solution of certain problems.

Thus, the library qualifies as a social agency or instrumentality. But the library is also humanistic in that its characteristics, modes of access to its resources, uses, and values are humanistic. It is not, and never has been, a scientific enterprise. Except for some tinkering with its processes, scientific technology has made but little contribution to the development of the library.

A catalogue entry on the face of a cathode ray tube is essentially the same entry devised by Charles A. Cutter, and the fact that it has been transmitted across the continent in a fraction of a second may be a convenience to the user, but it does not alter the character of librarianship or transform it in to a science. Of the importance of the humanities to a world of science, a professor of history at the University of Machine has recently written:

> "Our society is a seamless web, and ultimately science and technology share the same values and are dependent upon the purpose which derive from the study of what it means to be human. the neglect of the humanities will bring in its train inevitably the decay of science."

He goes on to characterizes an excessive dependence on science alone as

> "the higher barbarism, unless there is some human purpose that looks beyond the immediate technical and economic applications. The day will come when the hand will lose its cunning and life be found to be devoid of purpose. We are more dependent upon our poets than we realize."

It is perhaps reassuring that all of us know successful scientists who enrich their profession reading with generous additions from the humanities; who are accomplished mature musicians; or who, like the distinguished astronomer Fred Hoyle, have made reputation in creative writing.

Information theory is severely limited in its communicative potential. its only aim is to provide efficient access to knowledge, but the design of mechanisms, their production, and use of the system are its areas of concentration. We are, as Wright has emphasized, turning out control artists and data mechanics. This confusion of ideas with data can be dispelled only by distinguishing between data systems and idea systems. Thus, it follows that information science cannot qualify as a theoretical base for librarianship, and calling it bibliometrics or informatics does not alter the situation.

We librarians must constantly remained ourselves that our concern is with sociological and psychological phenomena, not physical objects and processes. Moreover, information science it self does not know what it is or where it is going. it cannot tell whether it belongs in a school of library science, engineering, management, operations research, or some loosely defined area of its own.

There is already distinct evidence that the American Society are of Information Science is fragmenting itself in to variety of activities, some of which are mutually contradictory. The term symbolic interaction refers to the process by which people relate to their own minds and the mind of others; the process by which individuals take account of their own or other's needs, desires, means and ends, knowledge, and like motivations. Among sociologists this phenomenon is frequently known as social interaction. In the definition of symbolic interaction, the word mind denotes instrumental activities that animals as well as human direct toward their environment. These instrumental activities, sometimes referred to as action or as psychological activities, are related to the organism's requirements and the conditions and resource in the environment that are relevant to meeting those requirements.

The term symbolic includes the representation of those requirements through a system of commonly understood linguistic, or other representational activates, such as gestures, where by the content of the communicated message is transmitted to, and understood by, the intended recipient. Such a discipline of symbolic interaction reminds librarians that their area of concern is based on social phenomena and it provides for the contributions of philosophy, linguistics, and psychology in the formulation of its unique purpose. That purpose is to make accessible the graphic records of human culture, so that people may understand the totality of the environment in which they find themselves and their own place in it. We who are librarians must constantly remind ourselves that information science is an area of inquiry, of research. It is not, as is librarianship, a service or a practice.

Information science can provide the librarian with some important and useful tools to expedite library service, but the ability to communicate a message with incredible speed over long distance through the use of glass fiber bundles or laser beams or to strove vat quantities of recorder knowledge in computer like mechanism does not in any way alter the purpose of the library. That the internal-combustion engine can move vat quantities of the library remains unchanged -to bring the human mind and the graphic record together in a fruitful relation for the growth of knowledge is still the goal.

Administration, management, architecture, and many other disciplines can contribute to the effectiveness of the library, but they are not librarianship. We who are engaged in library education must be aware that the librarian needs to attain certain specific skills in the uses of the tools that all these disciplines, including information science, have given us.

But the hard core of librarianship remains basically as it has always been-the mastery of the substantive content of graphic records. Librarians should be characterized by their knowledge and not by their instrumentation. The most effective librarians enter the profession armed with broad generalized knowledge or with knowledge in a substantive content of graphic records. The idea, not the process, is our primary concern. The great danger with which information science threatens librarianship is the loss of control of the library profession to other and less competent hands. Of the dangers inherent in this threat, we do not now seem to be fully aware.

The basic purpose of librarianship than is envisaged in the machine, and there is much more to librarianship than is envisaged in information science. If we permit ourselves to be mesmerized by the gadget. If we accept the flickering image of data on a fluorescent screen as knowledge, we will soon become like those mythical people of many centuries ago who mistook for the passing shadows reflected on the walls of a cave. So we conclude with the words of that distinguished librarian of Stanford and subsequently dean of the library school at Berkeley, Ray Swank:

> "The long experience and tested values of librarianship are still our most reliable and sophisticated resource for the solution of information-handing problems in most context whatever additional help may now be needed".

Two of the most prevalent impacts upon non-profit-making organizations, the sector to which most libraries and information centres belong, are increased demand coupled with reduced government support. These place increasing pressure upon managers to deliver more with less. The matter is further complicated as information is now regarded as a commodity or organizational resources.

Managers in public libraries and libraries attached to tertiary institutions are faced with the ethical issues and problems of providing free information services with dwindling resources where greater emphasis is being placed by government upon self-supporting or 'user pays' principles. Added to this is government pressure for greater financial accountability and for stakeholders to become increasingly more active in the operations of libraries and information centres.

Demands for lower personal taxation and increased privatization of many services influence how libraries and information centres are funded, structured and managed. Some types of library services will certainly be charged for in the future and methods of evaluating these and their relationships to the remaining 'free' services will need to be determined.In an effect to curtail expenditure it may not be easy to abandon services or levy charges. There may be enormous exit barriers to some services both on a social and economic scale.

Library and information centre managers may find themselves locked into many more programmes than they can afford. They will therefore need skills in polities lobbying and negotiating in order to secure the necessary resources in a competitive environment. Strategic planning and marketing skills will be aimed. A low coverage of too large a client market is inferior to a good quality service for a focussed market; and no library should be in the business of duplicating the services of other agencies.

Changes are occurring in the way in which libraries are evaluated. In the past, libraries have often been evaluated solely from a financial or economic perspective; that is, whether or not they have met their budgetary targets.

Today there is increased emphasis on measuring performance; that usually means efficiency and effectiveness. Meeting efficiency criteria involves the manager in value analysis; that is, ensuring that the optimum level of service is provided for the lowest possible cost something that all managers should be able to do.

However, the ability to meet the effectiveness criteria is not always as easy to demonstrate, since invariably the interests of stakeholder groups are not stable. Indeed, many have individual needs which they wish to be met, and which often defeat the concepts of economies of scale and efficiency.

Like most other organizations, libraries and information centres should have a corporate social responsibility, which involves satisfying the needs of the employees, public and community. This leads to the need for managers to integrate social objectives with the 'business' objectives in order to meet self-actualization and environmental demands.

One of the methods by which this can be achieved is by worker participation in management. Employees are increasingly becoming involved in corporate governance, and this involvement places greater emphasis on communication within the organization and the information-disseminating role of the manager so that employees are fully informed of the issues at stake.

Increased importance is being placed upon the quality of life. For libraries and information is being placed manifested in the quality of working life for the organization's employees and a higher standard of living reflected in changed consumer demand patterns for library services.

New values and structures are evident in society, which will not only be reflected in the demand for new resources but also in the work attitudes of staff and the corporate culture of the organization to which the library belongs.

Stakeholders are those persons who take an interest in the library, or who have the capacity to influence its ability to achieve its objectives. Examples of stakeholders for a special library operating in the private sector are unions, activities such as environmental, health and safety groups, shareholders or owners, political groups, suppliers, other libraries or information centres, employees and associations for librarians of information personnel.

Any of these stakeholders can have an effect upon the organization's direction by impeding or facilitating the accomplishment of the library's goals. Some have more effect than others, but the library or information centre manager cannot afford to ignore any of them, and all need to be managed.

This requires the library or information centre manager to identify who they are, their levels of influence and how each may politically, socially or economically affect the library's operations functions and future plans. These actions form part of an environmental analysis or situation audit. It is also important that the library or information centre manager ensures that sufficient resources are allocated to deal with them.

Over the past 10 years, libraries and information centres have been greatly affected changes in information technology, and the rate of change is still accelerating in this area. The introduction of the various changes in work patterns, demands for new skills, job retraining schemes and in some cases, a reclassification of positions.

Networking facilities have already caused managers to make new policies on interlibrary lending and reciprocal borrowing arrangements whilst it is anticipated that aspects of service delivery will change in the near future.

Library and information centre managers need to be aware of the penetration levels and rates of the new technologies in order to measure their effect on the delivery of services and operations of the library or information centre.

Strategic management provides a comprehensive approach to managing the impact of a dynamic environment upon the psychological sociological political and other subsystems which can be found in a complex organization. In so doing it considers the organization's functional and managerial ability to position itself to cope with a changing environment.

The strategic approach recognizes that an organization's long-term performance is affected by its strategic culture, managerial capability logistic capability and capacity, its technological thrust and its financial resources. These five features are critical to the organization's success. It loses any of these or they fall below a certain level or capacity the organization will cease to operate efficiently.

As a result it may lose its strategic position in the external environment and eventually disappear. Strategic management uses a planning approach, and as such requires the sanction and involvement of top management. Top management is also required to provide the knowledge and foresight to determine both the activities of the external environment, and the organization.

However, the planning process should also be a democratic people-interactive process. Whilst not everyone can be the planner, everyone should be involved to some extent in the top-down process. In planning for survival and success in a dynamic environment everything must be considered. The internal and external environment of the organization is studied, the results being used to provide input into the situation audit which evaluates the present situation. It may comprise of a strategic four-factor analysis, critical success factors, a SWOT (Strengths, weaknesses, opportunities threats) analysis or an organization capability profile.

The internal nature of the organization (Strategic culture, structure leadership style, technological thrust, and so on) should be evaluated with the external environment in mind. Financial and market analysis provide additional valuable information. Once all of the required information has been obtained strategies for survival can be planned.

Strategic management requires both strategic thinking and strategic planning and is a useful approach for managers as it enables the library or information centre to quantify and qualify its contribution to the community or organization on a long-term basis. It provides the opportunity for the library or information centre to justify its existence in other than financial terms.

7

Information Policies

Policy on the development of information services should be part of a nation's scientific, technical and economic planning and policy. Several developing countries have embarked on the planning of national systems or networks. Agency responsible for a national system or network of information services works with and advises executive and legislative bodies on setting up budgets, preparing legislation, and providing leadership for information developments. Usually, a substantial programme must be launched to build up the staff and strengthen the collections productivity centres, export promotion centres, development banks, central statistical institutes, book production centres, and the like. Such a national agency would also co-ordinate efforts with foreign assistance agencies, international agencies, charitable foundations and other voluntary organizations.

A national scientific and technological information policy can encourage the publication of the results of all indigenous, non-proprietary scientific and technical research, development, and applications. It can promote the co-ordination of data centres and library services and the improvement of abstracting and indexing services, translations and information transfer networks.

A national policy scientific and technological information should have the following general goals:

a) ensure the optimum utilization of accumulated knowledge in science, technology, economics, and social sciences in order to achieve national objectives for the betterment of society;

b) ensure the availability of adequate information for decisions for management and for policy both in government and in private enterprise.

c) focus the attention of governments and private organizations on the problems of information availability and use;

d) provide information services relevant to present needs, together with a capability for developing services to meet the future needs of generators, processors, disseminators, and users information and

e) promote national and international co-operation on the exchange of information and expertise.

Information systems of the future will probably exist within networks in which queries inappropriate to one system can be switched to another, in which specialized user requirements can be met by special adaptations, and in which experimentation and innovation can go on in parallel.

Unesco, in its feasibility study of a world science information system recommends the following strategy for a national information policy in developing countries: A national (or regional) agency should be established with governmental (or inter-governmental) support, for the purpose of planning for improvements in scientific information services, of promoting the growth of scientific library resources, and of developing a pool of qualified manpower. This would, in short, be a development agency, charged with the dual responsibility of increasing domestic resources, and of liaison, under the UNISIST programme, with foreign services. Where the geopolitical circumstances permit, this agency might well be regional rather than national in character, and be based on the voluntary co-operation of the independent governments in that area. A strong well-equipped library and documentation structure should be developed to provide necessary support for effective participation of the developing country in UNISIST.

While any developing country will of necessity turn to library resources external to the country for support, it is desirable to build and to organize reserves of heavily used books and journals, to inventory national holdings to develop interlibrary lending, and otherwise to strength the library functions. In preparation for adaptation to computer retrieval system of the future, the developing countries should see, through these national or regional agencies, that their information activities and procedures accord with international standards.

The design of a national or regional system of information services requires in the first place, an analysis of priorities in the economic and social, scientific and technical development of the country or region with studies of user needs and gaps in national information services and a decision on priorities in building a future system and services. These priorities will differ between countries and regions. The minimum activities of the proposed national system can be stated as follows:

a) provide basic services such as primary communication and publication channels; acquisition and collection of information sources, such as books, periodicals, patents, standards and other valuable literature, and exchange of these materials via interlibrary loan services with other information services, etc.;

b) perform the basic identification and location of information sources-union catalogues, abstracting and indexing services, etc.;

c) provide basic services in the dissemination of information by means indicated under (b), library services, translations, etc.;

d) provide depository services or clearinghouse services for local and external documents and data, important for the national development programmes.

Priorities can thus be derived not only from the subject fields but also the structure of services to be rendered, i.e., the emphasis placed on certain kinds of documents, exchange, translation service, etc.; One of the pitfalls of national priority-setting is the tendency to put the dissemination of scientific information before technological information services. This may happen because existing scientific information services are at a higher state of development and because of historical precedents in general.

In developing countries, with relatively low economic output, such a mistake could be extremely damaging. Information policy would result in little or no immediate improvement of economic and social conditions, causing a loss of support and possibly funds. No one model can be suggested for the determination of priorities.

But the list of priorities which was constructed in India in 1973 by an interdisciplinary planning committee, gives one example of actual priorities relating to economic development planning subject fields and information infrastructure. Priorities list for an Indian national science information policy.

1. Natural Resources Information and Data
2. Meteorology and Atmospheric information and Data
3. Rural and Urban Development Planning Information
4. Engineering and Industrial Information
5. Council of Scientific and Industrial Research complex Information Facilities Upgrading
6. National medical Library Facilities Upgrading
7. Patent Information Centre.
8. Statistical Information Centres
9. Promotion of Information Technology
10. Augmenting Facilities for Education and Training in information Science and Technology

Another way of establishing priorities is to itemize the problem for development and then determine what assistance can be gained for each from an information service.

For example, in Ecuador, the following factors were identified by CENDES (Centro de Desarollo Industrial del Ecuador) Technical Information Service as delaying the development of small Ecuadorian industry:

a) lack of an appropriate economy

b) deficient management practices

c) deficient commercial system

d) lack of market knowledge

e) low productivity

f) deficient technologies

An information policy for the development of small industry was formulated, to facilitate the transfer of technological information and to support efforts of technical assistance teams at plant level. Functions that could be performed by regional technical information services for small scale industries in Ecuador were grouped as follows:

a) collection and dissemination of economic and technical information, particularly that which is related to the identification and study of small industrial plants or artisan workshops which are economically feasible for establishment within the region;

b) application of new technologies or adaptation of technologies utilized in other regions;

c) standardization and quality control;

d) specialized technical counseling relating to processes, organization programming layout, design, working methods etc.;

e) management assistance and marketing assistance.

The work of the CENDES Technical Information Services has been important in the promotion of new industrial projects and also in the rationalization of production at installed plants. Technical information is disseminated by CENDES in the following fields:

a) rationalization of production,

b) identification of possible industrial opportunities of easy implementation

c) evaluation of technological alternatives,

d) assistance in the elaboration of feasibility studies,

e) creation of an infrastructure between the university, private enterprises and the state government sector.

The function of the state must be clearly set out at the beginning. The national system of information services must normally be based on binding legal provision for carrying out the main tasks. Responsibilities for control and advantagement of the national system of information services, planning direct allocation of funds, indirect financing by means of subventions and grants, methodological guidance etc., must be clearly defined. The role of governmental agencies in the sphere of information service is an important point.

Here Recommendation 15 of the above mentioned UNISIST feasibility Study may serve as a guide:

> "A governmental or government-charted agency should exist at the national level to guide, stimulate and conduct the development of information resources and services..."

Individual administration of sub-systems, though possible, is not likely to be efficient. But the UNISIST recommendation, though it can be met by such an arrangement, permits a variety of less centralized arrangements. UNISIST, as part of the Unesco programme, recommends the establishment of national focal points with policy and planning functions involving stimulation, financial support and co-ordination of information activities. but which governmental authority is the most suitable for the administration of these functions? No uniform model can be suggested; the solution must depend on the division of governmental functions in each country. Among the developed countries ministries which administer scientific research and/or technical development are usually also in charge of scientific and technical information. But different priorities in the overall development of a country may call for different solutions. For example in a country here a separate ministry? for research and development does not exist the focal point may be placed in the hands of another agency, for instance economic planning or education. Where administrative responsibility for science and technology is split, responsibility for information can go with either.

Once the governmental agency has been employed how can its administrative and coordination functions be made to work? It has been suggested that it should have a planning body with the following functions:

a) Planning and promotion:

elaboration of long-and short-team plans for activities, linked to other parts of the country development plan;

work on the promotion of the information system, technical and organizational projects, system analysis;

b) Co-ordination:

of activities of the documentation and data centres and library services to avoid duplication, e.g., the exchange services with partners abroad, translations, retrieval, etc.;

of training and education of information professionals and workers of the country; of research, development and design, serving the sphere of information services of international co-operation, contracts abroad;

c) Consultancy and advisory activities:

for governmental agencies concerning information services;

for governmental administration concerning legal acts important for the system of services;

in the field of methodology, standardization, classification;

on modern equipment (computing, telecommunications, reprographic equipment), modern methods of labour, design and construction if buildings for information services.

This body would not have to be big; it might even comprise a panel of experts from individual fields of information services with specialized knowledge and experience.

Representatives of the user communities-scientists, engineers, manages-could also be part of the staff of advisors. Such a body may as part of a ministry or other governmental agency, or be directly affiliated with the government.

System design of information services

The design of the system will be a painstaking and time-consuming task. For the elaboration of the design the assistance of international organizations and experts from developed countries may usefully be employed.

A system design for information services would be based on the priorities and would contain these main elements:

a) analyses of the information needs of the users, taking into consideration the present and estimated figures of potential users, their classification according to qualifications and specialization;

b) analyses of the present situation of library holdings and information services;

c) the design of the main links of the system which are to form a network in the country;

d) estimation of the number of personnel necessary for the system of services, classified according to the annual growth-rate, and qualifications, together with a plan for training both at home and abroad;

e) a design for the provision of space, material and techniques, with emphasis on correlations between the technical equipment and the individual links of the system-especially important when the computing, communication and reprographic technologies are gradually introduced;

f) a planning and development policy statement which would stress information policy objectives and cover legal and economic problems;

g) planning of financial means for the realization of the system, in which allocations both from the state and from other sources, e.g., industry or institutions, are combined;

h) creation of an activation mechanism, such as the establishment of a national focal point and a UNISIST national committee.

The system analysis carried out in close co-operation with the existing national, regional and international centres, would ensure that optimum use is made of his comprehensive preparatory work. The development of a network may involve close co-operation of several government authorities.

Networks would involve various levels of government authorities and private centres. In a smaller country, many of the functions would be performed by a single unit. The system design needs to tackle the problem of centralization and decentralization.

There is no generally valid model. The experiences of the developed countries show that the solution depends on many factors, but especially on the development of the country's structure and its political, social and economic systems. Each factor must be evaluated individually.

The UNISIST proposals for information policy Objectives stress the importance of this problem. The problem can be solved in stages. In the initial stage, when building up a system of services, a country will almost certainly establish a national centre or centres. In later stages, as the country advances its own scientific work, some of the services may be decentralized and specialized and/or regional centres may be established.

In the design of a national system for information services all links in the system (whether organizational or practical) would be integrated and clearly defined. The main links could be as follows:

a) state authorities for planning and co-ordination of the system of services in a country

b) a national centre (or centres) for data, documentation, and referral;

c) a network of specialized (subject or mission) information and data services which would be gradually built up according to the needs of economic, scientific and technical development; they could include state-run centres and specialized centres of private enterprises, industrial centres, of agricultural research, etc.;

d) a national network of information collections, either independent or integrated with other services that have lending arrangements to cover information needs in special technical and scientific fields;

e) service centres to handle specialized materials and primary publication services such as patent literature, standard literature, translations, etc.

The state authority for operation and planning is shown as a central agency on the highest level of government. The ultimate design for each country would depend on domestic factors.

In one structure suggested for the national information system the main link is a national centre. The tasks of such a centre, if set up, can be defined as follows:

a) acquiring and collecting information source in collaboration with the National Library. This includes establishing of collections of literature and data, i.e., important sources of information for science, technology, administration and economy, especially research reports and parent literature;

b) processing and evaluation of gaps in information sources, especially for the provision of secondary information and publication services (Central catalogues; indexing and abstracting services, data compilation, etc.) to meet the needs of scientific, technological and economic, development using collections to be found in the country itself and also foreign indexing and abstracting services; analysis of national and foreign literature received, preparation of state-of-the-art surveys on industry and comparisons of the level of national technique with the world-wide level;

c) dissemination of information collected and processed by means of bulletins, reference service, analytic reports, etc.; introduction of SDI (Selective Dissemination of Information Services);

d) advisory and referral services for data and other documentation centres, libraries, and users of information;

e) auxiliary and technical services in connection with the centre's own activities, especially translations, reprographic and other services for the domestic users of information;

f) methological work on the preparation of standards, guidelines, instructions, etc.;

g) research and development on information problems according to the needs of the country and the design of information systems;

h) training of information personnel (courses, travel abroad).

Each of these tasks are also explained in more detail. A glance at the table of contents will guide the reader to the more extensive treatments. In addition to these primary tasks, such a centre could publish regular and occasional information lists, bibliographies and compilation on specific themes such as information for the mass media about the state of development of the country. Such a centre could be the UNISIST focal point mentioned earlier.

The network of specialized information services and data centres in developing countries is undergoing gradual development. Special libraries are already established in most countries and are usually attached to government ministries or universities. Since special libraries play an important role in the integrated system of information services, the establishment of a network of these and other special information and data services is strongly recommended in the UNISIST proposals. Abstracting and indexing services, which help to cover national output of literature, and special services in the nation language can also form an important link in the national system of services.

Specialized information and data centres may be organized in different ways according to the system chosen and to local conditions. State-run centres (run as governmental agencies or those with State allocations) or non-governmental centres (run by industrial or agricultural associations or by universities) have each a role to play in certain conditions. The assignments of the specialized centres should be closely linked with the acquisition and collection of the relevant information sources in their subject fields. Each specialized centre should utilize relevant information sources abroad.

In developing countries by the availability and dissemination of data via data centres are, in general, handicapped by the isolated locations of these centres and their low production of national data. At present most scientists are obliged to search personally for the data they need and spend considerable time and effort in doing so. In some developing countries the potential production of useful data is high, particularly in parts of the life and earth sciences, but such "reservoirs" of data are underdeveloped.

These data, if available, would be useful to their own countries as well as of value to scientists throughout the world. In such cases, it is desirable for the countries concerned to launch programmes for systematic observation, collection and dissemination of relevant data; in this way might establish closer contact with the world scientific community and receive the necessary impetus to activate local scientific research. In order to realize this, however, they would need appropriate financial and scientific assistance from international or national organizations. In any case, it is very important to improve the accessibility to, and dissemination of, data for scientists and other users in developing countries.

Information about global data referral centres, such as the Nuclear Data Centre of the U.S, Atomic Energy Commission, needs to be provided to groups of users in these regions. In the design of data dissemination services in developing regions, it is particularly important to estimate user needs and data productivity in the region.

The following main types of relations between data centres, information services, and library networks have been found:

a) an independent data centre network and an independent library network under the guidance of different governmental offices;

b) an integrated data, information library network under the same supreme authority or under different by co-operating authorities;

c) documentation activity included in the library network;

d) library activities included in the data and information service network;

e) library network without data and documentation networks.

A special government department could be set up to the administrative and technical centre of the country's libraries. It might operate in the ministry of education, the national library or some other location that would enable it to cover all levels of activity. In countries with a federal structure, library service departments may also be needed in states or provinces.

In a country where the library services are extremely underdeveloped, a centralized library planning office may also centralize certain library technical services such as various aspects of selection, acquisition, cataloguing, classification, arrangements for audio-visual equipment and its distribution, organization of public information services, library co-ordination and the supervision of publicly provided library services.

In this case a highly competent technical staff is needed in addition to the library planning staff. Parts of the network of national library services would include:

a) public libraries

to serve as a centre of culture and information in the community;

to provide services for all sections of the community;

to encourage and promote the use of books and information.

b) university libraries:

the prime function of a university library is to contribute towards undergraduate and postgraduate study programmes as well as the research programmes of the university. This, however, is not its exclusive function. A university is generally supported by public funds and its libraries represent a substantial part of the total library resources of the nation. It is incumbent on the university library that these resources should be made available to everyone through an integrated national library network.

c) school libraries

the basic purpose of a school library is to make books and other reading material available to teachers and pupils in support of the teaching programme and to further the general intellectual development of a student, playing an active part in the educational process, persuading staff and students to read and use information sources, guiding them in their reading and information seeking.

In a developing country the essential tasks of a national library are:

a) complete collections of the national literature and literature on the nation;

b) depository and/or copyright functions;

c) national bibliographical services;

d) national and international exchange of documents;

e) maintenance of national union catalogues.

The need for co-ordination of the functions of a national library network with those of a national centre must be stressed. This applies in particular to the establishment of collections, the complication of catalogues and the organization of the relevant reference and referral services.

Many of these comments would also apply to the centres holding special material such as patents, translations, standards. A complete design for a national system of information services cannot exclude these special collections.

The development of information services means long-term cost-intensive investments which yield the result-"information"—only after a comparatively long starting period. As the financial situation, the priorities, the number of available trained personnel and the attitude of those responsible for decision making differ in each country, we do not suggest a uniform model but name some of the most important to be considered when financing the projects.One of the decisive facts is the limited resources of developing countries and the consequent emphasis on economy in the establishment of their system of information services.

The need for technical assistance from international organizations and the industrialized countries needs to be emphasized. This assistance can successfully bring the information services of a country to life, and may also help in the designing of information systems and the acquisition of expensive equipment.

The actual operation of the national system of information services, however, should be solely in the hands of the country and should be covered by the country's own financial means. In many countries the provision of information relating to development will be considered of sufficient public value for the service to be given free of charge; the full cost will then be borne by the government.

There are good arguments against free information services: usually information received free of charge is not criticized but accepted even if it proves valueless and inaccurate. Nevertheless, in countries where there are few users for particular services, the running costs may be so high that many users refuse to pay the price and so forego the information. Government aid is therefore inevitable.

The cost of establishing and operating information can be defrayed from the following sources:

a) governmental subsidies,

b) assistance from international organization,

c) assistance from foundations and other private organizations in or outside the country,

d) payments from users,

e) payments and donations from groups or projects having high demands for data,

f) bilateral assistance from governments.

Any of these options can be combined in order to cope with the financial burden. Along with government support, foundations and private organizations seriously concerned with the encouragement of science and the utilization of the results could give some appropriate support. So could academic and research institutions and learned societies. Without subsidy, evaluated data services may have to be marked at much higher prices than document or bibliographic information services. Yet it may be impossible for university research workers to use these high-priced services. Just as nobody expects the price of scientific journals to cover the cost of the research from which the papers have resulted, it can be argued that prices for data-dissemination services need not cover the cost of computers etc.

Effective operation of the various components of a national system of information services requires that specialists of many kinds should be available-subject specialists, information professionals, system designers, and others. Once policy has been set, operations are carried out by those specialists who are most effective for the tasks performed. However, all tasks that require judgement on the value of information in a given field must be made by someone of adequate education and training. This principle cannot be stressed too strongly. Plans for a build-up of the requisite personnel should form a permanent element of the system design. Such plans should include;

a) medium term plan with provision for annual growth;

b) the qualifications required of the personnel- graduates, undergraduates, others;

c) summary of the foreseeable demand for training personnel for specialized centres in agriculture, industry, medicine, etc.

The introduction of computer-based information services requires the following provision:

a) realistic approach to the use of computers for data, documentation and information services, based on computers already installed for other purposes such as administration and research;

b) transfer to computer methods by a comprehensive step-by-step process, based on an analysis of the existing data bases, the economic feasibility of running them and the training of personnel;

c) a sufficient computer capacity in the country, and technical assistance in computer applications oriented toward data and information services;

d) a telecommunication capacity for data transmission from other countries which have information services of value to the country's national system.

Unequal rates of progress in computerization have widened an ever-growing gap in development of information services. Nevertheless, machine-readable materials need not be inaccessible to any country.

They can be accessed by means of world-wide information services. International efforts are of great importance in this area. Once telecommunications systems permit the reliable and economic transfer of data and information around the world, a new era will have arrived. In readiness for this certain development, preparation within a country should be made along the lines suggested here.

Reprography is another technique for information service which is of the utmost importance for the developing countries. It can also be introduced immediately. No lengthy technological training is called for and the use of each piece of equipment produces immediate results; moreover, the investment is rather modest. Reprographic equipment of the most recent type must be acquired.

The development of international co-operation and the establishment of international and regional information systems are characteristic features of the present stage of development of information services. In addition there is a rapid increase in the number of specialized materials, the development of electronic data processing and of computer-based indexing and literature-searching services, the introduction os SDI systems, etc.

Efficient national systems provide a solid basis for international co-operation. Interdependence between national and international system calls for extensive co-operation of the technical and methodological sides of information-systems planning.

Some aspects of international and regional co-operation are:

a) co-operation with the specialized agencies of the United Nations and other international organizations;

b) implementation of the technical assistance programme of the international organizations;

c) co-operation concerning the utilization of the technical assistance offered by developed countries;

d) participation in the international UNISIST programme.

In some cases several developing countries have joined to form regional centres on a common linguistic, geographical or geopolitical basis. Regional programmes can be made to work along with the existing national systems. They can be the focus for joint activities.

The range and method of these activities will depend on the conditions in which the regional group operates. The efforts of Nordforsk in Scandinavia FID/CLA and OAS in Latin America, and FID/CAO in Asia are worthy of note as they provide for exchanges of information on current activities and plans. Regional programme can perform the following functions:

a) joint research and development, experimental testing of new equipment, methods, etc.,

b) co-operation or research, development and experimental work, elaboration of new designs for documentation and library activities in the countries concerned;

c) co-operation and/or joint training of information personnel, particularly the higher forms of training.

d) joint subscription to the large indexing and abstracting services;

e) joint acquisition and joint use of expensive information sources;

f) additional translation services for languages other than English and French;

g) co-operation of use and methodology of computer systems.

The regional centres should be firmly anchored in the international arrangements of the countries concerned in which the tasks and the contributions of the respective countries, the principles of joint administration of the centre, the principles of appointing staff members and control of their activities are defined. Co-operation with international organization working on data and information services may significantly help to develop the national services. Many international organizations try, within the framework of their activities to improve the implementation of national systems for information services in developing countries.

Many international (governmental and non-governmental) organizations are concerned, too, with a elaborating and evaluating suggestions and designs for the improvement of the transfer of information to developing countries. There are several ways of linking developing countries with the information systems of the regional organizations and the international organization of the United Nations family such as UNIDO, ILO and FAO.

There is interaction between the information exchange of centres from developing countries and the above-mentioned organizations. There are activities of some international governmental and non-governmental organizations, such as the organization for Economic co-operation and Development (OECD), the International Federation of Documentation (FID), the International Federation if Library Associations (IFLA), and others which assist developing countries in their efforts.

The establishment of information services in developing countries through technical assistance can be an important part of the permanent programme of international organizations particularly the specialized agencies of the United Nations.

In many cases, this is already done, but some countries have not yet fully realized the value of such assistance and have not requested it. The management of such technical assistance requires an integrated information policy in the country being assisted. International assistance can be expected to become very important for the management of national information systems.

The United Nations system, bilateral aid agencies from of a national developed countries and various international organizations consider strengthening of a national system for information services as a priority, but there is a concern that international projects should be followed up and should not collapse, as they sometimes do, after the departure of the foreign expert.

UNISIST is a programme in which Unesco strives to create a world network of information services based on the voluntary co-operation of existing and future national information systems. It plays a facilitating role in assisting countries in the formulation of information policies. Full-scale action on the UNISIST programme started in 1973. In the 1971 feasibility study undertaken jointly with ICSU, Unesco launched the idea of the UNISIST programme to serve the scientific and technical community in all member countries.

Developing countries have since emphasised the need to meet urgently the information requirements of their entrepreneurs (farmers, manufactures, etc.). The UNISIST programme goals now give due consideration to this technological aspect for developing countries. At the 18th session of the General Conference in 1974 decision was taken to gradually extend the UNISIST programme to social sciences. The flexible programme objectives of UNISIST include:

a) co-operation of existing trends towards co-operation acting as a catalyst for the necessary developments in scientific and technical information;

b) synthesis of diverse philosophies programmes, and policies that relate to the free flow of scientific and technical information, in order to stabilize and co-ordinate existing trends towards international co-operation in the communication of scientific and technological information.

c) making the products of information systems exchangeable from one system to another by establishing UNISIST working groups which can develop the necessary common standards, rules and procedures;

d) with full compatibility between all information systems as a long-team goal, provision for the development and collection of conversion programme between systems with a view to establishing interconnection between systems that are not directly compatible;

e) action to strengthen the functions and improve the performance of the institutional components of the information transfer chain, such as libraries documentation centres, indexing and abstracting centres, information analysis centres and numerical data centres;

f) assistance in promoting the collection critical evaluation organization and dissemination of numerical data; development of general procedures of data handling and evaluation; investigation of the special needs of the engineering profession for data compendia; and compilation of a world-wide multidisciplinary inventory of existing information analysis centres;

g) ongoing national and international assistance programmes for training and education in the field of scientific and technical information with other United Nations agencies, competent professional organization, scientific unions, and funding organizations;

h) regional pilot projects to assess effective approaches to linking existing information facilities is science and technology in various into operating networks.

The ultimate objective of the UNISIST programme is to provide different user groups, especially in developing countries with improved channels of access to the world stores of scientific and technological knowledge for the overall benefit of mankind.

As far back as 1972, the United Nations agency UNDP, selected the linking of knowledge institutions to local productive sectors and the access of these sectors to world scientific knowledge as two main elements needed to promote the technological independence of developing countries. With financial assistance from UNDP.

UNESCO is responsible for informing policy-makers of advances in the management of national information systems that may serve their countries social and economic objectives.

Developing countries that understand the need to strengthen their information infrastructure express their need for assistance to UNDP, though other UN agencies handle the assistance projects.

Multi-purpose information institutions, such as interdisciplinary libraries, receive their assistance through Unesco. Specialized agencies of the UN family assist the development of specialized information systems.

The Food and Agriculture Organization of the United Nations (FAO), for example, assists in the development of agricultural information systems within the framework of the International Information system for the Agricultural Sciences and Technology (AGRIS), and the United Nations Industrial Development Organization (UNIDO), in the development of industrial information systems. In addition, Unesco has convened in September 1974, an intergovernmental Conference on the Planning of National Documentation, Library and Archives Infrastructures.

Re-affirming the recommendation of this Conference, the general Conference of Unesco, at its 18th session, invited Member States to take suitable action to create or improve appropriate national infrastructures of documentation services, libraries and archives (NATIS), in accordance with the economic, social and cultural structure of the country.

It invited the Director-General of Unesco to promote this concept of planning national infrastructures of documentation, libraries and archives and to draw up a programme, taking into account UNISIST and other relevant international programmes, for submission to the 19th General conference of Unesco. Important assistance in this sector of information institutions is also coming from many sources besides the United Nations family.

Developed countries, through bilateral aid and international organizations such as the International Development Research Centre (IDRC) in Canada and the German Foundation for International Development, are joining their efforts to build national information systems.

Both bilateral and international sources of assistance can show surprising responsiveness when approached on a "personal" basis with precise requirements. Efforts to provide developing countries with improved to the world's information resources may bring practical results sooner than one might expect. Already well defined information services are appearing in fields of practical interest and are available for common usage.

Index